THE SCHOOL CONNECTION

THE SCHOOL CONNECTION

Parents, Teachers, and
School Leaders Empowering Youth
for Life Success

Sheila E. Sapp

ROWMAN & LITTLEFIELD
Lanham • Boulder • New York • London

Published by Rowman & Littlefield
An imprint of The Rowman & Littlefield Publishing Group, Inc.
4501 Forbes Boulevard, Suite 200, Lanham, Maryland 20706
www.rowman.com

86-90 Paul Street, London EC2A 4NE, United Kingdom

British Library Cataloguing in Publication Information Available

Library of Congress Cataloging-in-Publication Data

Names: Sapp, Sheila E., author.
Title: The school connection : parents, teachers, and school leaders empowering youth for life success / Sheila E. Sapp.
Description: Lanham, Maryland : Rowman & Littlefield, 2021. | Includes bibliographical references. | Summary: "The theme of the book is about the importance of collaborating and partnering among parents, schools, and community stakeholders to empower youth for life success."—Provided by publisher.
Identifiers: LCCN 2020048609 (print) | LCCN 2020048610 (ebook) | ISBN 9781475854664 (cloth) | ISBN 9781475854688 (epub) | ISBN 9781475870145 (paper)
Subjects: LCSH: Education—Parent participation—United States. | Parent-teacher relationships—United States. | Community and school—United States. | Communication in education—United States.
Classification: LCC LB1048.5 .S27 2021 (print) | LCC LB1048.5 (ebook) | DDC 371.19—dc23
LC record available at https://lccn.loc.gov/2020048609
LC ebook record available at https://lccn.loc.gov/2020048610

♾️™ The paper used in this publication meets the minimum requirements of American National Standard for Information Sciences—Permanence of Paper for Printed Library Materials, ANSI/NISO Z39.48-1992.

To all parents and students who passed through the doors of Woodbine and Crooked River Elementary schools during my tenure as principal. I am forever grateful for the experiences and friendships gained that helped me develop into an effective teacher, mentor, and school leader.

Train up a child in the way he should go: and when he is
old, he will not depart from it.
—Proverbs 22:6 King James Version.

CONTENTS

FOREWORD

Who would be better to write a book about success than one who has passionately dedicated her life to improving the lives of others? There is no doubt the author, a not-so-retired school administrator, has the knowledge, skills, and background to communicate how parents, teachers, schools, and communities can build success among our nation's youth. How is that? Forty-plus years of education and experience from the classroom to a wide range of administrative positions provided opportunities for her to understand and value the parent and school connection and the expertise to define and pen this piece of work.

I have known this author, Sheila Sapp ("Sheila E. Cares" in her consulting business), for more than thirty years. It was always Dr. Sapp in the work world, but the friend I've come to know is simply called Sheila. This bundle of energy was raised in New Jersey, and from the time she started learning how to help students, she hasn't stopped.

My first encounter with Sheila was in an attempt to gain a teaching position in the district in which she was an administrator. In time, we became fellow principals, and eventually I worked closely with Sheila while administering several local, state, and federal programs. Our conversations during the early years were mostly work- or task-related, but as time passed, I began to deeply appreciate the woman, both personally and professionally, who would soon become someone whose genuine aspirations, motivation, and desire to improve the lives of others was awe-inspiring.

In June of 2017, Sheila retired as an elementary school principal only to launch immediately into writing her third book, entitled *Staying the Course*, which was a masterful guide for aspiring and current school leaders. Sheila's social media posts and live videos demonstrate her high levels of energy and enthusiasm for life. Her inspirational quotes, as well as thought-provoking questions, are examples of her many ways of reaching out to friends, parents, former coworkers, and school personnel for the sole purpose of providing information, inspiration, and encouragement to others.

I remember leaving the hospital with my newborn. As soon as the nurse closed my car door after baby, daddy, and I were loaded, I felt an overwhelming sense of panic. I wanted the nurse to come home with me! Of course, that didn't happen. I thought I was fairly well read on the how-tos of being a new parent but wasn't prepared for many of the adventures that awaited me. This book is much like the manual I wish I had owned in those early years. It defines what is important and provides practical insights and tips for helping youth become successful in life.

Like I wanted a full-time nurse that first day at home, long ago teachers realized they needed the support of parents in order to best develop a successful learner. Sheila describes the importance and benefits of parents being engaged in their children's education as well as the benefits of teamwork between teachers and parents. Most importantly, Sheila shares how to effectively build partnerships and meaningful engagement among parents and the school community, which lead to better attendance, grades, and school completion, as well as better socialization and fewer discipline problems. Of great benefit is her focus on parents of special needs children. Practical roles and tips for building relationships and improving roles as team members and for individual education meetings are provided.

Some of the best parts of this book are the simple tips and recommendations Sheila has created for making home settings conducive for learning; explanations of key roles; rationales for certain rules, regulations, and guidelines; following protocols; and her Power Tools for success, which focus on building self-confidence, self-esteem, resilience, and perseverance. She includes actual Power Tool games and easy-to-do instructional activities along with instructions and material lists.

Sheila Sapp has done it again! Her unwavering commitment to the success of children and youth is revealed throughout this book. Those who are committed, especially parents, to investing in the lives of our youth and who want practical, easily understandable, and implementable strategies and tips for improving the parent/teacher/school connection should read this book.

Beverly S. Strickland, EdD
Retired teacher, principal, and director of
federal programs and projects

PREFACE

As a recently retired educator with more than forty years of experience working directly and indirectly with parents/caregivers, the gradual decline of parental and community involvement throughout the years became a genuine concern for me. Parents have always been key influencers for their children's attitude about learning and school. Researchers validated the impact that their support and involvement had on academic achievement and school success.

This manuscript is also a fulfillment of my long-term goal to write a resource handbook specifically designed to share information about schooling. A resource book is needed to ease the adjustment and transition of parents/caregivers who are entering the educational setting for the first time. Since involvement and family engagement are decreasing, school administrators and teachers should actively recruit parents/caregivers and community stakeholders. The skills and expertise of parents/caregivers and community stakeholders will enhance and expand schools' current repertoire of resources used for school improvement.

ACKNOWLEDGMENTS

I am grateful for the continued support and encouragement of my husband, Everette, and my daughter, Dr. Nicholyn Hutchinson. Their suggestions and recommendations help refine my ideas and improve communicating with the public.

INTRODUCTION

The importance of parents partnering with their schools to promote academic achievement and overall well-being for children and youth is a proven fact. A plethora of research has emphasized the role parents play as key people in their children's education. By strengthening the bond and relationship between parents, teachers, and school leaders, we can equip children and youth with tools to handle our ever-changing society. Researchers also cite the relationship between home, school, and community as the key to addressing the school dropout issue and increasing the number of motivated students.

Despite convincing evidence concerning the positive impact of parents' involvement with their child's/children's education, there are still parents, policymakers, and community members who view school and student learning as the sole responsibility of educators. Educators, however, know they can't close the academic gap and raise the achievement for all students alone. School leaders and teachers need the support and assistance of parents as well as the community to obtain school goals and meet the specific needs of each student. It truly does take a whole village to raise a child.

Parents, however, tend to lessen their involvement and engagement with their child's/children's education and school as they move up in grade levels. There is a drastic drop in parental involvement and engagement once their children reach middle school. As a matter of fact, decreasing parent participation is one of the biggest problems schools face today. The trend is for schools to reach out to parents and develop programs that will assist them in garnering parent buy-in and community support. Additionally, many current grant programs such as Title I require parental participation as a component of the grant.

State and federal grants require school systems and schools to allocate a designated percentage of approved grant funds to address specific parent needs and activities. Grant administrators closely monitor all expenditures related to parental engagement/involvement activities. Parent engagement with their child's/children's education and academic achievement are encouraged and linked to school system and school level goals. School administrators are expected to annually report progress/growth attained on goals and academic achievement to staff, parents, and other key stakeholders in the community.

During the review of literature and informal sessions with parents, I noted that parents have a marginal understanding of what school leaders do and what it takes to run effective, high-achieving schools. Also, school leaders are struggling to maintain and increase parent engagement in their schools. Some parents, however, judge schools based on their own experiences with schools as children and occasionally view schools as unfriendly, confusing, frustrating, and bureaucratic in nature. Culturally different parents are very reluctant to engage with their children's school due to language barriers.

There is still a need to clarify the role of principals and demystify *schooling* for parents/caregivers. It is imperative that schools continue to explore ways to enhance the engagement of parents and community stakeholders to obtain their support in the quest of meeting the academic, emotional, and social needs of our youth. Parents and community resource services are valuable resources that can augment what's available in schools. Regardless of the educational setting parents/caregivers choose for their children, the educational journey is daunting and intriguing. Parents, however, are still needed to promote children's/youth's academic growth and progress.

I wrote this resource book to encourage parents to reconnect with their children's schools and to strengthen the relationship between the home, school, and community. Another goal is to provide parents/caregivers with a guide to help them understand the underlining rationale for selected rules, procedures, and policies that are often sources of frustration and confusion for parents or caregivers. As an added feature, select chapters have tips, recommendations, strategies, and questions to encourage discussion and reflection, as well as simple, easy-to-do instructional activities to help parents/caregivers navigate *schooling* and ensure future life success for their children/youth.

As a former school leader and classroom teacher, I experienced first-hand the impact parents have on children's growth and achievement. I also witnessed and experienced a steady decline of parents being involved or engaged with their children's education, teachers, and schools. Even with the onset and increase of technology and development of communication software programs, we still have parents who shy away from being involved or engaged with schools. Family dynamics have changed drastically over time, and youth needs have steadily increased. Schools need to continue to tap underutilized parent and community resources.

This resource book is organized to enable readers to select a chapter based on specific needs or areas of interest. Additionally, each chapter will conclude with a section titled *In Review*, summarizing key points and highlights of information presented. Additionally, the topics discussed and explored in the resource handbook apply to organizations outside of schools such as churches, child-care centers, Head Start programs, Boys and Girls Clubs, Girl and Boy Scouts, youth groups, and recreation centers that serve families and their children.

Current staff and school personnel may use this resource handbook as a tool to explore, examine, and brainstorm/generate proactive ways to address parent concerns and to implement effective engagement programs/activities. Enlisting the support and utilizing the talents, skills, and input of parents/caregivers and community resources will enhance and strengthen schools' pursuit to obtain school goals, promote growth for all students, and close the achievement gap among subgroups. A strengthened and improved bond between the home, school, and community will broaden the narrow road to life success for youth.

I

PARENT INVOLVEMENT

It's Evolution

Parents' involvement with their children's education is not a new phenomenon. Prior to the 1850s and before the development of public education in America, parents were totally responsible for their children's education. With the advent of public-school education, standardization of curriculum, and the growth of professionalization of teachers, parents are no longer the primary source to educate youth. What role do parents currently play in their children's intellectual, social, emotional, and physical development? How can parents, schools, and the community partner to empower youth and ensure life success?

A HISTORICAL PERSPECTIVE OF PARENT INVOLVEMENT: IN THE BEGINNING

A child's education was totally under the purview of his or her parent or family. All educational activities were conducted privately by parents rather than through public institutions. During the early history of America, colonists had local control of their children's education and schools. Religious leaders of the day created schools that centered around different religious and moral beliefs. Early curriculum focused on discipline, work skills, ethics, and the teaching of values. Lay citizens who were parents in the community and members of lay boards managed and supervised the schools.

Public education and the spread of public schools in the late 1800s and early 1900s impacted parental education responsibilities. Additionally, as teacher professionalism and standardization arrived on the educational front, parents began to believe that professionals alone should be responsible for educating children. The arrival and influx of immigrants made it mandatory and necessary to have trained instructors *Americanize* these new citizens, enabling them to become viable and contributing members of this growing society. Parents began to allow professional teachers to educate children.

Although the control and major responsibility for educating children changed hands as public graded schools increased, parents were still considered valuable resources and encouraged to be involved with their children's schools. Early teachers saw the importance of parents helping children at home. As a matter of fact, parental involvement has been a concern of educators and concerned citizens since the turn of the twentieth century in the United States. In 1897, an organization founded by Alice McLellan Birney and Apperson Hearst called the National Congress of Mothers planned and held their first convention in Washington, DC, on February 17, 1897.

As social activists, they were not only concerned about women's right to vote, but they also wanted better conditions and education for children who were finally allowed to go to school instead of being victims of *cheap* child labor in sweatshops and factories. On that eventful day in February, they hoped for at least a gathering of two hundred mothers to discuss the plight of children and education. Surprisingly, more than two thousand people came, consisting of mothers, fathers, doctors, and lawyers to discuss their concerns for children. Birney and Hearst were overwhelmed with the support and interest of individuals from all walks of life focused on bettering children's lives and their education.

A document emphasizing the organization's purposes—"education of parents for child development; the cooperation of home and school; the promotion of the Kindergarten movement; the securing of neglected and abused children; and the education of young people for parenthood"— was developed during the convention.

Selena Sloan Butler founded the National Congress of Colored Parents and Teachers (NCCPT) in 1926. Modeled after its white counterpart, the National Congress of Mothers, Selena Sloan Butler also became its first national president. Mrs. Butler dedicated her life to uniting home and school into a planned program for children. The National Congress of Parents and Teachers and the National Congress of Colored Parents and Teachers merged into the National Parents and Teachers Association (National PTA) to serve all children in 1970.

Although the National Congress of Mother's document was written more than 122 years ago, as a nation, we are still proponents and supporters of utilizing parents to help improve student learning. Years of research studies support the impact of parental involvement. Schools need strong, meaningful, and vibrant parent participation to impact student achievement to make substantial academic gains. Through advocacy and family/community education, the National PTA established programs and called for legislation to better children's lives with programs, such as:

- creation of kindergarten,
- child labor laws,
- public health service,
- hot and healthy lunch programs,
- juvenile justice system,
- mandatory immunization,
- arts in education, and
- school safety.

The African proverb "It takes a village to raise a child" still rings true for today. Parental involvement has taken on a renewed cloak of importance. Schools more than ever need not only parents but also community organizations and concerned citizens to help obtain and accomplish school improvement goals. In recent years, parent involvement acquired a renewed role. Parents have moved from simply being room mothers, volunteering in classrooms, chaperoning, and conducting fundraising projects to more inclusive approaches. School-family-community partnerships consist currently of mothers, fathers, grandparents, caregivers, foster parents, relatives, retired individuals, stepparents, business leaders, and community groups.

Researchers cite parent-family-community partners as key for addressing problems such as school dropouts and unmotivated students. Involved school-community partnerships also help foster higher educational aspirations and reduce disconnected youth. Additionally, regardless of a parent's educational background, social status, and family income, parent involvement affects the academic achievement of minority students across all minorities. A broad-based effort in all communities will aid schools in closing academic gaps that exists between minority and special needs students. Supporting students throughout their education includes addressing students' social service needs too. Exactly what types of support are needed to effectively assist schools?

Parent involvement means different things to different people. Many schools are using a research-based framework developed by Joyce Epstein consisting of six types of parental involvement. They are: parenting, communicating, volunteering, learning at home, decision making, and collaborating with the community. This wide range of activities enables schools to extend their parental involvement activities and engage all parties in helping them meet the needs of their students. Following is a detailed listing of Epstein's framework with a brief description of the six parental activities:

- Parenting: Assist families with parenting skills, family support, understanding child and adolescent development, and setting home conditions to support learning at each age and grade level. Assist schools in understanding families' backgrounds, cultures, and goals for children.
- Communicating: Communicate with families about school programs and student progress. Create two-way communication channels between school and home that are effective and reliable.
- Volunteering: Improve recruitment and training to involve families as volunteers and audiences at the school or in other locations. Enable educators to work with volunteers who support the school and students. Provide meaningful work and flexible scheduling.
- Learning at Home: Involve families with their children in academic learning at home, including homework, goal setting, and other curriculum-related activities.
- Decision Making: Include families as participants in school decisions, governance, and advocacy activities through school councils or school improvement teams, committees, and other organizations.
- Collaborating with the Community: Coordinate resources and services for families, students, and the school with community groups,

including businesses, agencies, cultural and civic organizations, and colleges or universities.

Although researchers have emphasized the importance of parental and community involvement in accomplishing school goals and impacting student learning, there are parents who see their children's education and learning as the sole responsibility of teachers. Other parents, however, cite roadblocks or barriers that keep them from volunteering their services to local schools such as their personal work schedules, feelings of inadequacy, language barriers, negative past school experiences, lack of resources or skills to work with their children, and frustrations with school bureaucracies and policies. These hindrances, whether perceived or real, can limit students' and schools' growth.

Homeschooling and the number of homeschooling parents have increased rapidly along with dissatisfaction with public school's curriculum and standards, which have focused more on academics and less on the social, emotional, and character development of children. Many families have elected to have more control and say over what their children experience or are exposed to daily. With the assistance of online curriculums, resources, and supplemental materials, homeschool parents design an educational setting and instruction for their children that align closely with their values, principles, and religious beliefs. They hold firm to their right and responsibility to educate their children without professionally trained teachers.

Schools are overburdened with cries for academic excellence and unrealistic demands of parents. With the added changes due to the breakdown in family structures, schools find themselves being held responsible as the venue for solving many parent issues and concerns. To aid and assist working parents, many school systems have implemented before- and after-school programs to *babysit* before and after school. Two-parent families have declined. Families are overwhelmed with trying to survive in today's economy. Volunteering or getting involved with their children's school or education is not a high priority.

Educators need to place an emphasis on reaching out to parents and their stakeholders in order to respond effectively to the rigors of maintaining annual growth for all students in their schools. It is going to require total commitment and active planning to engage parents and community stakeholders. Some school leaders are satisfied with the low turnouts for events at their schools if they can document they have offered an opportunity. They can check off that a meeting was held for program or grant requirements.

School leaders and teachers can't assume that low or no attendance at school-sponsored meetings is an indication that parents don't care. Teachers and principals need to understand that there are many reasons why parents and community stakeholders don't get involved with school and their child's/children's education. Until school administrations try to have open dialogue with parents, they'll never find out or understand what the barriers are that hinder parents from coming to school. As educators, we are aware of and talk about the changing family, but are we attuned to their specific needs?

School leaders should ensure that discussions about family and community involvement don't focus on the lack of participation from families. Some teachers spend time sitting in lounges discussing and sharing the inadequacies of parents. They have no interest in trying to find out what selected parents could offer or contribute to their classrooms. They often claim that parents/caregivers who need to come never show up. This attitude represents a deficit model for involvement that assumes that parents need to participate so teachers can *fix* them. Teachers with this view see remediation, not collaboration, as the reason for involving parents.

School administrators are also guilty of having a deficit model for involving parent/caregivers in their schools. Like teachers, some principals neglect to take the time to build relationships with parents/caregivers or community stakeholders. They rely heavily on a select small group of PTA parents to spearhead fundraising projects and other events to purchase supplemental materials and equipment for their building. They don't spend time building relationships with their parents and community stakeholders. Surveys and questionnaires are sent out sporadically to solicit input or feedback from their parent clientele.

Results of their surveys and questionnaires are used to plan *required* parent engagement activities to meet grant guidelines. Responses that are received from parents and community stakeholders, however, are *not* used to help develop and design activities and programs to meaningfully engage parents. In some instances, feedback/input or concerns expressed by parents or community stakeholders are perceived as attempts to *run* the schools. Also, occasionally teachers think a parent who questions classroom rules or homework policy is trying to *run* the classroom. There needs to be a meeting of the minds.

School leaders and teachers need to take the first step to recruit parents/caregivers and community stakeholders. To start the process, school administrators must be purposeful about the mission of engaging parents and community stakeholders. By strengthening the connection between the home, school, and community, a powerful network of services can be created. This network will be able to ensure all social, emotional, physical, and intellectual needs of every student are met. Achievement gaps will close. No one will slip between the cracks.

CHAPTER I SUMMARY

Parents' involvement with their children's education has evolved over time from total control to less control and responsibility. Despite changes, parents/caregivers are still needed and considered a valuable and effective resource. Currently, school communities are strongly encouraged and expected to partner with parents, concerned citizens, and community resources to help solve social and academic needs. Schools can no longer operate as islands unto themselves and obtain school goals and close achievement gaps.

Parents/caregivers and community stakeholders are a powerful untapped resource for schools. School leaders must be front-runners in recruiting and engaging parents and community stakeholders for the betterment of their schools. Schools are not able to effectively meet annual mandated achievement targets without utilizing all resources that are available to them. It is time to engage parents and stakeholders in ways that will cultivate buy-in and create advocates for schools. School administrators and teachers need to adjust and realign their thinking about nonattending or nonparticipating parents.

Efforts need to focus on soliciting input and feedback from parents to help schools be attuned to the needs of parents and community stakeholders. There are a variety of reasons why parent attendance and participation are waning in schools today. Low attendance in schools does not mean there is a lack of concern or noncaring parents. We as educators need to lead the effort to garner feedback and input from parents to strengthen our connection and collaboration with them. Additionally, there are varied definitions of what parent involvement is and what it looks like. School systems and schools are encouraged to *engage* parents to have *viable* partnerships.

Parents'/caregivers' involvement with their children's education is vital for children's educational journey. Parents/caregivers are needed to support their children's learning in the home. It is important for teachers to collaborate and partner with the parents of their students. Parents foster and nurture children's desire and love for learning. The foundation they lay at home for learning and thinking provides children with a roadmap for success. Parents also are experts on their children and can offer information that teachers can use to supplement what they know about children in their classroom.

Chapter 2 will examine and explore meaningful different roles parents perform in schools. Following a discussion of parental roles, I share benefits children receive as a result of their parents' participation and involvement at home and in school. I also present issues and strategies recommended to strengthen the school-family-community partnerships. There is a brief discussion about barriers to parent involvement and the difference between *parent involvement* and *parent engagement*.

Exactly what roles do parents play in classrooms and in schools? Why are some parents/caregivers reluctant about collaborating with their children's teachers? What can school administrators and teachers do to ease fears and feelings of mistrust? How can school administrators and teachers serve and engage parents and community stakeholders effectively? These questions and concerns are addressed in the upcoming chapter.

2

PARENTS' ROLE IN EDUCATING YOUTH

It is a well-known fact that parents are key players in guiding and overseeing their children's education. Many parents, however, do not realize how important their role *is* and how they lay the foundation for their child's/children's learning journey. They can promote children's healthy intellectual, physical, and social-emotional development. All these factors are vital for preparing youth for school and ensuring academic success. The plan for building a positive and supportive foundation for children should start at birth and progress as children mature. How do parents begin this process? How can they influence children's learning?

Parents start the learning process for children by beginning with themselves. Children spend their early lives listening to significant people in their lives—their parents. According to Kelly (2019), parental engagement with their children's education needs to start early to support academic achievement. Youth learn who they are and whether they are loved through what they hear and experience. How they see the world and view their immediate environment depends on the adults or significant caregivers children interact with daily. It is paramount that parents provide an environment that encourages the development of a love for learning.

Parents and caregivers can begin the process of developing a positive learning environment for children by taking an objective and sincere look at themselves. They need to remember that who *they* are today is based on the environment and experiences faced during their childhood. Even their thoughts about learning, school, and education are the result of past experiences and expectations. Following are a list of questions formulated to help parents and caregivers to ask themselves to assess where they currently are. Honest and sincere responses will assist parents/caregivers in designing a supportive environment.

Creating an Environment to Foster Learning: Self-Assessment

- How do I learn best or my preference? (kinesthetic, visual, auditory, or tactile)
- What is my temperament?
- How do I approach challenges?
- Do I always see the glass half empty or half full?
- Do I believe you can learn from mistakes?
- Do I value education?
- Am I a lifelong learner?
- Am I patient and tolerant?
- How do I view failure?
- Am I open to new or different ideas?
- Am I open to constructive criticism?
- Am I supportive?
- Do I encourage exploration?
- Am I curious?
- Do I have high expectations?
- Am I interested in learning?
- Do I provide a variety of meaningful educational experiences for my child/children?
- Am I resourceful and creative?
- Do I support learning at home? If so, how?
- Am I currently involved with my child's/children's learning?

After responding in writing to the above questions, take time to reflect and evaluate your responses. Are there any questions you struggled with? Were you unable to pinpoint exactly how you felt about a question or two? Don't be discouraged or disappointed because of your lack of certainty. There are many resources available online to assist you in further developing areas in which you feel less adequate or knowledgeable. It's important to focus on your strengths and areas needing growth to create the best learning environment possible that'll put your child/children on the path to a healthy and successful life.

Every parent faces the dauntless task of providing appropriate educational experiences that foster intellectual, emotional, social, and physical development for youth. Many parents embrace their role through home-schooling and/or involvement with the schools their children attend. Others shy away from serving as role models and designers of their children's intellectual development and passion for learning. They may not be aware of how important and substantial the knowledge they pass on is to their children's development.

In May 2016, the US Departments of Health and Human Services (HHS) and Education (ED) issued a joint policy statement on family engagement from early years to early grades recognizing the critical role parents play in promoting children's success. The report supported an earlier study that found parent engagement led to:

- higher grades and test scores and enrollment in higher-level programs,
- increase in earned credits and promotions,
- improved attendance,
- improved behavior and social skills, and
- increase in enrollment in postsecondary education.

Additionally, the Every Student Succeeds Act (ESSA), an educational reform plan, replaced the No Child Left Behind Act in 2015 to help parents understand educational policy at the local, state, and federal level. ESSA emphasizes the importance of stakeholder engagement. States are mandated to have input from the community. States, school districts, and schools must solicit and evaluate parent input when developing strategic plans for schools. Schools are currently seeking ways to connect with parents to achieve outcomes that will assist them in increasing academic achievement and obtaining district- and school-level goals.

Another research study (2017), *Unleashing Their Power and Potential*, reported a surprising finding concerning parents' perception about education and their elementary-age children. They are more concerned about their children's happiness than academics. Additionally, parents of elementary-age children begin being more concerned about their happiness and well-being, but these priorities shift in middle school when preparedness for postsecondary school becomes a concern. Schools experienced a drop in parental involvement and engagement as children move from elementary to middle and high school.

Many of the research studies about parent involvement also show the elementary level of schooling is the best time for parents to explore the world of learning with their children. Children can be exposed to a variety of fun and helpful learning activities such as cooking, gardening, reading, exploring the outside world, visiting museums, and so on. Participating in meaningful activities reinforces children's interest and desire to learn new things. Some parents, however, think it's the teachers' role to teach, not theirs. This belief limits a children's educational development and potential. Youth *learn* all the time.

Parents should continue to be involved with their children's schoolwork as they get older. Benefits of early parental involvement in their children's learning behavior are:

- Parents and children enjoy a deeper interaction.
- Children who receive assistance at home tend to do better on standardized tests.
- Children show improved self-esteem, self-worth, confidence, and behavior.
- Children complete homework more easily and consistently.
- Parents are more aware of what their children are learning and can pinpoint areas or subjects in which the children may need additional help.

They need to accompany children/youth on their educational journey to ensure they are on course and not distracted or dissuaded from their academic potential. Parents should view themselves as the *builders* of their children's educational development. Parents or caregivers who are *builders* don't see schools as having the total responsibility for educating their children. They understand and value collaborating with teachers and schools to learn how to provide additional academic enrichment opportunities in the home. Parents, like general contractors, are the directors of their children's education from preschool through college.

Parents/caregivers are children's *first* teacher. Whether they realize it or not, all parents serve as learning role models for children. As children grow and develop, their parents' role evolves. Their attitudes and perceptions of learning and education can inspire children to take charge of their own educational journey. When children are young, parents have a strong lead and presence in their intellectual life. Once children enter formal school, parents can show children how exciting and interesting learning can be. The learning that began at home between parents and children can be extended to schools and classrooms. Also, parents can help children connect everyday life to school and world events.

The aforementioned joint policy statement issued by the Health and Education Departments recognized and supported the importance of strong family engagement in early childhood programs and systems as central to promoting children's healthy intellectual, physical, and social-emotional development. Parents are viewed as a source for preparing children for school and supporting academic achievement from elementary school and beyond. As a result of research-based studies on parent engagement, schools are seeking to involve parents as partners to help raise achievement.

By paying attention to how their children learn, knowing their interests, and practicing what is learned in school at home, parents/caregivers strengthen the home connection and obtain a deeper understanding of their school's improvement goals. Parents' newly acquired understanding is an asset for schools soliciting honest parent input and feedback. Their participation as viable contributors will assist schools in meeting all the needs of their students and parents as well. Other strategies parents can employ to fulfill their role as active and involved learning models for children are:

- Know and keep abreast of academic standards and grade-level expectations that must be reached for each grade level.
- Monitor homework, support child/children, answer questions, and help only when needed.
- Review and check classwork, quizzes, assessments, projects, and assignments daily.
- Observe child/children while working on assignments at home and note difficulties.
- Contact classroom teachers immediately to share areas of difficulties or questions about assignments.
- Keep lines of communication open and positive between home and school throughout the school year.
- Encourage children to do their best every day.

- Show your support and interest for what's happening in school by asking questions about your children's school experiences.
- Help your child/children take charge of their own learning by setting academic and personal goals.
- Keep television watching and electronic device usage at a minimum.
- Don't overschedule your child/children with extracurricular activities.
- Serve as a learning model by learning something new yourself.
- Help prepare them for tests.
- Provide a pleasant learning environment and atmosphere for learning at home.
- Give constructive criticism in a positive and encouraging manner.
- Reward children appropriately for good results on tests and assessments.
- Take educational trips on holidays or breaks that are related to classroom learnings to increase understanding and supplement classroom instruction.
- Involve children in active learning in their neighborhood and/or community.
- Devise and plan fun ways to review learnings at home.
- Share some of your school experiences with your children.
- Make sure your children get proper rest at the end of the day after study and playtime.
- Set aside time to talk with your children and have meaningful discussions about their school experiences, issues, or concerns.
- Attend parent meetings and other appropriate opportunities to interact with the school and children's teachers.
- Be a good friend and sounding board for children to share their thoughts, ideas, and true feelings.
- Set aside time to read to your children and encourage them to read with you also.

Many parents and caregivers do make the effort to work collaboratively with their children's teachers and schools. They accept their role as learning models for their children who thrive. However, we still have parents who for various reasons and factors have very little to do with their children's education and schools. In some cases, families may be dealing with challenging issues such as divorce/separation, homelessness, job loss, language/cultural differences, and health issues. School leaders will have to face these challenges and develop/implement strategies to meet the needs of their struggling parents.

Kelly (2019) recommends that school leaders and teachers who want to have meaningful dialogue with parents to design viable parent involvement/engagement activities should survey parents to improve communication. The key suggested survey questions to improve conversations with parents are:

- What values do you believe are essential for a developing child?
- What part of the current curriculum is essential?
- What should we be teaching that we are not?
- What skills will they need for the future?
- What role would you like to play in the education of your children?

Adams (2020) contends that research shows the best way to engage parents is not to talk at them but to provide a welcoming, warm, responsive, and listening environment. Parents are drawn into true meaningful partnerships with family get-togethers and involvement in hands-on curricular and instructional activities. During these family get-togethers, teachers and school administrators share information about what's happening in classrooms and how they can support learning at home. Instead of schools using parents as customers for fundraisers, parents are treated as important members of their schools' instructional team.

Throughout the country, school systems are designing and implementing different creative ways to harness the support and skills of one of their most powerful resources—parents. Schools can no longer expect to draw parents and other stakeholders without concerted efforts to build solid relationships and true partnerships with their parents and community members. Families have a variety of needs, issues, and concerns. For schools to enlist their support and help, they must find ways to gather and utilize parents' valuable feedback to gain their trust and participation. What part do school leaders and teachers play?

EDUCATIONAL LEADERS' AND TEACHERS' ROLE IN ENGAGING PARENTS AND THE COMMUNITY

Educational leaders and teachers are challenged annually with the task of increasing students' academic growth and achievement. As the instructional leaders in their buildings, they are responsible for designing and implementing improvement plans to ensure all students with different ability levels will progress. To meet the challenge of providing continuous growth and meet school improvement needs, school leaders need to utilize a variety of instructional materials, programs, and other resources.

By engaging parents and appropriate community stakeholders, school administrators and teachers will be able to use the skills and expertise in the community to help accomplish system- and school-level mandated academic targets. Schools are already facing the challenge of declining parental involvement or parental engagement. Instructional leaders along with their teachers and other staff will need to design and plan meaningful activities and events to increase buy-in support from parents and the community. It's essential for schools to implement parent/community partnerships.

According to Sanabria-Hernandez (2019), for schools to effectively engage their parents, they must know their specific needs and concerns regarding their children's learning transitioning from one grade and/or educational setting to the next. To engage stakeholders in the community, however, school leaders need to showcase their school's academic growth and challenges annually to parents and community members. Every effort needs to be made to post and/or advertise events and accomplishments using social media and other forms of communication. Plan activities for parents and community members to garner support.

Teachers and other appropriate school personnel can join school leaders in planning and implementing strategies to engage parents and the community to build and foster buy-in. School administrators can't build partnerships with parents and the community without commitment and support from their school staff. Therefore, the first important and critical step is to build a staff by hiring competent people who support the school's expectations and know how to work collaboratively with parents and the community. Educational leaders need to also periodically provide up-to-date training on effective communication.

Following are tips recommended by Sanabria-Hernandez (2019) for teachers to use to *draw and attract* parents to schools to become partners:

- *Make the most of drop-off and pick-up activities.* Take advantage of this opportunity to greet parents in a special way, acknowledge their arrival, and ask about their well-being. If they stop by the classroom, have the class say, "Good Morning," and say, "This is [student name]'s mother [or father], class." Find out if they have any hobbies or special interest. Be warm and welcoming always.
- *Share a detail or two about their child/children. Provide brief specific information.* "Johnny did a good job reading his sight words during reading group time today!"
- *Host a lot of activities.* Plan activities in conjunction with your grade level—Donuts with Dad, Muffins with Mom, Grandparents Day, etc.
- *Communicate frequently.* Contact parents with good news as well as issues or concerns. Parents love to learn about what is happening in their child's/children's classroom via newsletter, flyers, e-mail blasts, telephone calls, handbooks, bulletin board class newspaper, social media, videos, teacher webpage, etc.
- *Celebrate achievements through work sampling.* Create portfolios, booklets, or scrapbooks, and post work in the classroom or set up displays in the community.
- *Encourage peer networking among parents.* Create a contact list for parents to network with other parents in the class. Make sure other contact numbers are listed that may be needed by all parents. Be sure to get parent's approval of having their contact information publicized first.
- *Identify and make useful resources available to parents.* Try to have resources available to help parents who may have questions about the school's student behavior policy/procedures, dress code, grading policy, subject matter/curricular concerns, standards, etc.
- *Invite parents to your classroom.* Be sure to frequently invite parents to your classroom throughout the school year. Invite them to be silent observers or active participants.

Teachers are key ambassadors for recruiting parents for schools. They need to develop and build relationships with students and their parents.

By being friendly and welcoming, teachers can set the tone for the type of relationship they want to have with parents. Generally, most parents want the best learning environment for their child/children. Children and parents who feel they are accepted and cared for as people thrive in nurturing environments. Building relationships with parents and students does not happen overnight. Additional activities or ways that teachers can build relationships and recruit parents as partners are:

- Share personal information and pictures that tell or display who they are as individuals, such as their children's and husband's names, where they are from, their hobbies, and so on.
- Do a neighborhood walk and get to know the areas where their students live.
- Find out the interests and extracurricular actives of their parents and students.
- Share briefly trips or weekend activities with the class and parents.
- Be respectful and accepting of culturally different parents and students.

Engaging the community is another resource that educational leaders need to capture and utilize to assist with their school improvement and academic achievement goals. Exactly how do school leaders enlist the support, participation, and buy-in of community stakeholders? In 2017, Wood and Bauman, along with the Freddie Mae Foundation, published a study on four school districts that had implemented family and community outreach programs.

They found four foundational elements of the programs had an impact on positive parent and community partnerships and collaborations. They were:

- active nurturing of respectful and trusting relationships,
- school leaders who are supportive and engaged in partnership efforts,
- skilled staff that work to align and coordinate partners, and
- using data to set priorities and then act upon them.

School administrators understand and have learned how difficult it's been to recruit and engage parents for their support. Engaging community stakeholders requires additional efforts. It's recommended that sharing school data is an effective strategy to solicit support and feedback from community stakeholders. Publicizing data and sharing concerns informs community stakeholders and parents about the current status and specific needs of the schools located in their community. To assist school administrators with school improvement projects, community stakeholders must know schools' needs to offer viable feedback and input.

Community stakeholders' access to data helps them determine how they may work with the schools in their community. Also, school leaders benefit from feedback from community stakeholders to enable them to modify/adjust current engagement programs to address concerns of their community partners and make decisions. Schools have the responsibility to train and show their community stakeholders how to interpret and compare data with other schools. Community stakeholders have a stake in the future and need to know if schools in their community are excelling and what skill areas need improvement for progress/growth.

To gain interest of community stakeholders partnering with schools, communication between schools and community stakeholders must travel both ways. School administrators can share their data and find out about concerns stakeholders may have about the local schools in their community. People want to know how the students are performing. This exchange of data and information encourages and fosters support, buy-in, and ownership of local schools in the community. Additionally, community stakeholders can share the resources and expertise of their organizations/businesses with students and school personnel.

According to Bernhardt (2003), there are four types of data schools need to share with the community to help them gauge the effectiveness of their local schools. They are:

- demographic data that describes the school (safety, teacher turnover rate), students (class size, race, dropout rates), staff (years of experience, certification), and community (economic base, growth projections);
- student learning data that shows the impact of the education system on the students (standards assessments, teacher-assigned grades);
- perception data that helps schools understand what stakeholders think about the learning environment (student perceptions about what motivates them to learn and teacher perceptions about what kind of change is possible); and

- school processes data that helps build a continuum of learning for all students (instructional strategies and classroom practices).

By aggregating the above data and sharing it with their community stakeholders and parents, schools can portray an accurate picture of their learning environment and student performance. For successful and effective feedback and engagement from community stakeholders, educational leaders need to ask questions such as what data they are interested in, what concerns they have about the school, and what data they are interested in seeing that shows improvement. Also, letting community stakeholders know how their input and feedback impacted school improvement plans strengthens partnerships and collaboration.

Listed below are a variety of ways educational leaders can solicit community stakeholders' feedback and begin and engage in meaningful dialogue:

- Host open public forums
- Distribute community surveys and questionnaires
- Host focus groups
- Have individual conversations with community stakeholders
- Host study circles
- Create social media groups

It is imperative and essential for educational leaders to find ways to connect and build relationships with their community. By doing so, they can provide and ensure the best learning environment and resources for all students. Sharing their data with the community fosters productive and relevant conversations and promotes support.

CHAPTER 2 SUMMARY

Chapter 2 focuses on the important and critical role parents play in the education of their children. Research studies' findings on parent involvement and engagement support the benefits and the need for schools to utilize this viable resource. Parents who can have meaningful and productive interactions with their children at home assist schools in obtaining schools' improvement and achievement goals. Parents and caregivers are also provided with questions to encourage thoughts about learning, which can be used as a tool for determining strengths and areas needing development.

The learning needs assessment serves as a guide to assist parents in implementing a stimulating learning environment for youth. Additionally, parents/caregivers gain an idea and understanding of what constitutes a positive and supportive learning environment and ways to strengthen the home-school connection. Parents are viable and effective learning models for their children. By working collaboratively with teachers and schools, they can assist schools with closing the achievement gap among different ethnic groups. To meet the needs of all students, schools need parents'/caregivers' support and involvement with their children's learning.

Parents and community stakeholders are valuable resources for schools. Educators know they are not able to close achievement gaps, accomplish school improvement goals, and meet all students' needs alone. There is a continuing need for schools to actively not only involve parents and the community but also engage parents/community through meaningful and rewarding partnerships. There is a discussion about the role school leaders and teachers must play to recruit and solicit parent/community input and feedback. Strong partnerships can be fostered and nurtured through planned family- and community-friendly programs and events.

Successful and vibrant parent/community partnerships can serve all their students and families. By using the input/feedback from parents and the community, schools can modify and adjust their programs to meet the concerns and needs of their stakeholders. Additionally, schools promote and encourage buy-in and ownership of their schools through viable partnerships. They tap into the expertise, resources, and skills of parents and community stakeholders that extend and enhance their repertoire of school improvement strategies. School leaders can ensure academic achievement, growth, and success for *all* students.

3

PARENTS/CAREGIVERS OF SPECIAL NEEDS YOUTH

Survival Tools

Children vary developmentally, physically, emotionally, socially, and intellectually. There are parents who have children who need additional services to address specific needs and disabilities. Special needs students have individualized education programs (IEPs) that are developed by school personnel, special education teachers, and other specialized staff to meet specific disabilities. For parents new to special education services and the process, IEP meetings can be overwhelming and daunting.

Parents/caregivers of special needs youth face heightened challenges and responsibilities when compared to their counterparts. Not only are they key in providing education, but they're also charged with the task of requesting appropriate supplemental services and/or resources. In many instances, special needs children, depending on their exceptionalities, need additional services in order to function and progress based on their abilities. It is always important for parents of special needs children to be focused and tuned into their children. Empowering and equipping these parents is a continuous challenge for all educators.

I have chosen to present and discuss a variety of subjects/topics in chapter 3 emphasizing their importance for parents/caregivers of special needs children. Although I recognize and believe that all parents need to be involved with their children's education, it is a critical issue for parents who may have additional emotional, social, physical, and intellectual deficiencies to handle and address. Additionally, many of the topics shared are informative and applicable for teachers and school leaders. Therefore, references for teachers and school administrators will be dispersed when appropriate throughout the chapter.

ESTABLISHING RELATIONSHIPS WITH TEACHERS AND SCHOOL LEADERS

Parents/caregivers need to make establishing a positive relationship with their child's/children's teacher a number one priority. For their child/children to have a successful and rewarding school experience, teachers, school administrators, and other school personnel need to be familiar with the child and parent. Occasionally, parents/caregivers aren't forthcoming with information about their child/children for a variety of reasons. For some, it may be their way of not facing or accepting the fact that their child/children does need additional support or special education services.

Others may have experienced mistreatment or negative consequences in the past as special education students. In instances of this nature, they are very guarded and don't want their own child/children to experience what they did as students. Or they just don't want their child/children to be treated differently. There have been many changes with special education, and people in general are becoming more accepting and knowledgeable. There is an increased demand for inclusion as special education students' least restrictive environment. Parents are demanding and wanting their children to learn with peers in the same classroom.

The key resource tool parents need to share with the classroom teacher, school leader, and other appropriate school personnel is the child's/children's individualized education program (IEP). Parents should not assume that teachers always receive a copy of the IEP or know what accommodations or modifications they need to make to assist with the learning. Take the time to meet them prior to school start, if feasible. Share as much information as you can about your child's/children's personality and how he/she learns best. No one knows your child/children better than you. Connect with your child's/children's school.

INDIVIDUALIZED EDUCATION PROGRAM (IEP) PARENT AND CAREGIVER TIPS

The most important conference parents/caregivers of special needs children have is the individualized education program (IEP) meeting. Whether you are new to special education or a veteran, it is important for you to be an active participant in the process throughout your child's educational journey. Some parents may be overwhelmed by what takes place when they meet with a team of professionals. It can be very intimidating being surrounded by *experts*. Parents/caregivers must remember they too are *experts*. Their knowledge and information are as valuable and significant as the other data presented.

IEP meetings can still be a source of confusion and frustration at times for parents who aren't new to special education. Listed below are questions Morin (2018) recommends for parents to ask to help them be more confident as a member of the IEP committee and better prepared for their child's/children's individualized education program meeting. Questions to ask before, during, and after IEP meetings are as follows:

Questions before IEP Meeting

1. What is the goal of this IEP meeting?
2. Can we create an agenda for this meeting?
3. May I have a copy of my child's current IEP document to follow along as we are talking in the meeting?
4. Could you please provide me with prior access to copies of notes/reports we'll be going over?
5. Who at the meeting will be qualified to interpret the results of my child's independent educational evaluation?

Questions during and/or after IEP Meetings

1. How does everyone at the meeting know or work with my child?
2. Can you tell me about my child's day so I can understand what it looks like?
3. Can you explain how what you're seeing from my child is different from other children in the class?

4. Could we walk through the current program and IEP plan piece by piece?

5. How is my child doing in making progress toward his/her IEP goals?

6. What changes in goals would the team recommend?

7. Is this a SMART (Specific, Measurable, Attainable, Realistic, and Time-bound) goal?

8. How is this goal measured and my child's progress monitored?

9. How will my child be assessed according to grade level?

10. Who will work with my child? How? When? Where and how often?

11. What training does the staff have in this specific intervention?

12. What does that accommodation/instructional intervention look like in the classroom?

13. What support will the classroom teacher or teachers have in putting these accommodations/interventions into place?

14. What can I do at home to support the IEP goals?

15. I'd like to see the final IEP before agreeing to any changes suggested at the meeting. When can I see a copy?

16. When will the changes to his/her program begin?

17. How will we let my child know about any program changes?

18. Can we plan for keeping in touch about how everything is going?

19. May I have a copy of notes the teacher referenced during this meeting?

20. If I have questions about the information given about my child's rights, who is the person to contact to call another meeting?

In addition to recommending questions for IEP meetings, the items below are helpful items to have during meetings:

1. an IEP binder;

2. a notepad to take notes;

3. a partner, advocate, or friend to take notes (note: inform the IEP team in advance);

4. an audio recorder or smartphone app if you'll be recording the meeting (check with your state's Parent Training and Information Center regarding policies about recording meeting);

5. the current IEP;

6. a list of questions you want to address;

7. an IEP goal progress tracker, progress reports, and report cards;

8. work samples that illustrate progress or concerns;

9. notes about strategies that do or don't seem to be working at home;

10. proposed accommodations and suggested SMART goals;

11. any private evaluations you want to share;

12. evaluations reports from your child's most recent school evaluation(s);

13. school contact sheet to update with new provider information;

14. parent-school communication log or other notes about phone calls, meetings, or e-mails to or from school;

15. a letter of parent concerns to attach to the IEP, listing your child's strengths, areas that are challenging, how your child is doing in and feeling about school, and other things you'd like noted;

16. tissues (IEP meetings can be emotional sometimes);

17. a bottle of water (nerves and talking can make the mouth dry); and

18. a collaborative mindset.

At the conclusion of your child's IEP meeting, you will leave with a draft copy of the program (IEP) plan developed. After arriving home, reread and review the draft IEP document carefully. Make sure you are satisfied with the academic and/or behavior goals. Go through and underline or highlight any wording or ideas you are uncertain about, don't understand clearly, or disagree with. If you are not satisfied or have a change you want included, contact the appropriate special education personnel and/or school-level administrator. As a parent/caregiver, you have the right to request changes or disagree.

Occasionally, parents/caregivers may feel pressured into agreeing with or accepting the individualized education program drafted for their child/children. They must guard against this feeling. Parents need to make sure they don't compromise their beliefs and concerns for their child for the sake of having a timely meeting or appeasing others in the meeting. Children should always be the main priority and focus of every IEP meeting held. Anything less than what is best for a child is a detriment to his/her intellectual development, potential, and access to a free and appropriate education.

Morin (2014), offers eight IEP dos and don'ts for parents to follow during a meeting. These rules of IEP etiquette are good for parents, teachers, school administrators, and other IEP team members. They are:

- DO be respectful of other people's opinions. Being rude or attacking a person for his/her opinion will not be helpful in coming to an agreement. It's more likely to make other people defensive and not willing to listen to your opinions.
- DON'T accept opinion as fact. Feel free to ask for clarification or for the evidence that backs up an opinion.
- DO ask questions. If there is something you don't understand, speak up. You're probably not the only person around the table who doesn't understand what's going on to make informed decisions about your child's education.
- DON'T be intimidated. Staying silent because you are worried about what other people will think or because you think the professionals know best will likely lead to resentment and misunderstandings.
- DO give people the benefit of the doubt. Making accusations or assumptions that the school is going to oppose your ideas just because they can isn't fair. Unless you have a clear reason to believe otherwise, it's better to assume that everybody there wants to help your child.
- DON'T be accusatory. Even if you encounter differing opinions or opposition, try to stay firm but fair. Until you ask directly about the motives behind a decision or opinion, you can't know for sure what somebody else is thinking.
- DO keep your temper. It's okay to be emotional in an IEP meeting, and it's even okay to cry; most people will be sympathetic and understand that it is difficult to sit in a meeting and hear about your child's weaknesses. But it's essential to keep your temper under control. It may not be easy to do especially if you feel like your parenting is being questioned, you're not being listened to, or an inaccurate picture is being painted of your child. But losing your temper may also cause your point to be lost as well.
- DON'T hesitate to disagree. If you think a goal isn't appropriate, you have the right to say so. If you think a teacher isn't seeing the full scope of your child's limitations, speak up and explain what

other teachers have seen in the past and what you see at home. Disagreement doesn't necessarily have to cause strife. It's a way to make sure all the issues and angles are thoroughly explored.

Another safeguard to protect the overall purpose and effectiveness of the IEP meeting is the words that are used by parents and other participants during the meetings held. Knowing how to use your words to express your opinions, concerns, or issues in an appropriate, respectful, and professional manner is a necessity. The presentation of and terminology used can influence the way or how an idea or suggestion is received or accepted. If you disagree with a program suggestion or decision, carefully choose your words.

For example, parents should say they think a specified program is an *inappropriate* program for their child rather than say it's not an *ideal* program. Or, if they disagree with an educational setting offered, say *an inappropriate educational setting* rather than it isn't the *best educational setting*. Morin (2014) believes parents/caregivers who express themselves carefully and clearly by using appropriate wording demonstrate their awareness of the Individuals with Disabilities Education Act, 1975 (IDEA). Its basic requirement is for individuals to be provided and given an appropriate education.

Additionally, choosing your battles during these IEP meetings is another point for parents/caregivers to consider. Sometimes you can shoot yourself in the foot or make your cause less important by *fighting* over and questioning everything whether it is significant or not. Parents should avoid getting the reputation for being difficult or known for making unrealistic requests from school systems, classroom teachers, school administrators, and schools. School systems do not earn the same amount of funding, and what one school system may be able to provide as a supplemental service may not be feasible for another school system.

There is nothing wrong with giving your opinion and asking questions appropriately. Make sure your questions or requests focus on what is appropriate for your child. Morin (2014) warns parents about administrators or teachers making assertions to head parents off at IEP meetings. These assertions are blanket statements that are presented as facts without proof of their accuracy. Assertions parents/caregivers may need to listen for that might surface at an IEP meeting are:

- That service/program costs too much.
- We must consider how child's disability/behavior is affecting the education of other children in the classroom.
- Providing that service for your child means that another child will have to go without services.
- That's not a service we provide.
- We're not allowed to discuss that.
- It's our policy to do it.
- That's just the way things are.
- That's not the law.
- As a general rule . . .

There is no logical evidence to back up the above assertions although they sound like they are backed with authority. It's appropriate for parents/caregivers to ask questions and request additional information (proof). If you are facing a challenging statement or decision, ask to receive a copy of the policy, regulation, or rules. There is nothing wrong with seeking confirmation from individuals at a higher level. Be direct and nonconfrontational. Always focus on what is appropriate for your child's/children's education—your main goal.

Remember, no matter how pressured you may feel to agree with a plan presented at your child's IEP meeting, you have the right to disagree and refuse the plan. Also, you have the right to request your disagreement or concern be documented in the minutes of the meeting. Never sign an IEP document with incomplete information. Make sure that whatever you want added or deleted is done. It is good operating procedure to carefully scan the document for correctness and accuracy. Be certain that the completed IEP reflects what was discussed and recommended during the meeting.

Finally, even after you sign your child's/children's IEP, you can change your mind about the program and/or your child receiving services. Submit a letter in writing and contact your local special education director or coordinator to complete the appropriate form.

Once the IEP is signed, everything should go forward and be implemented as planned. What if you notice after the plan has been implemented for several weeks that things are not being carried out in your child's classroom as discussed and documented in the IEP? You are disappointed in the school and the teacher. What is your next step as a parent/caregiver when processes and procedures are not going on as planned? What other options are open to you? Is there a procedure in place to address violations? You have expressed your concerns, and the classroom is refusing to comply with the IEP requirements. Is there another step?

Teachers and schools *not* following IEP guidelines and procedures is the most prevalent cause of a breakdown in collaboration, cooperation, and partnering with parents of special needs youth. Do not assume teachers have a copy of a child's IEP. Contact the classroom teacher and find out if he/she has a copy of the document. Also, having a copy of the IEP doesn't guarantee he/she knows how to follow the recommended accommodations. The first step is to make an appointment and meet with the classroom teacher to find out what the issue is and why the IEP isn't being implemented correctly in the classroom.

If there isn't a satisfactory resolution, contact the school administrator and/or appropriate special education personnel. There are additional guidelines to follow if you need to go further. As a former school administrator who has worked with teachers and parents of special needs youth, I can reliably say it is imperative to follow the levels of communication specified. Everyone wants to have the opportunity to resolve an issue or problem when it is brought to their attention. Nothing destroys an established relationship quicker than a parent/caregiver, teacher, or community stakeholder going over your head.

COMMUNICATING AND COLLABORATING WITH PARENTS OF SPECIAL NEEDS YOUTH: TIPS FOR TEACHERS AND SCHOOL LEADERS

Being a member of an IEP team can be an important role and responsibility for school personnel. It is a task that can be viewed with a positive outlook if you have the right perspective and understand and know how to relate to the parents of special needs children. There are some educators who are closed-minded and are unwilling to learn how to communicate with parents/caregivers in general. Parents of special needs youth need to be handled with patience and care. As a matter of fact, all parents should be treated with upmost respect and concern regardless of their children's intellectual potential or possible handicaps.

Although new and veteran teachers and school administrators receive training or have sessions during undergraduate/graduate classes on building relationships with parents, there is still a need to continuously renew or provide additional training. Communication is an area that benefits the entire organization. Many school- and district-level initiatives and goals are obtained successfully when communication and relationship building are valued highly. All parents/caregivers want their child loved and cared for by his/her teacher and other school personnel. They are more cooperative when teachers accept their child for who she/he is.

The tips specified below are simple to implement and assist teachers and school leaders with communicating and relating authentically with parents of special needs youth as professionals and IEP team members.

Navigating before IEP Meetings: Early Preparations

- Get to know the parents and other team members before the scheduled meeting, if feasible. Review and become familiar with prior assessments results administered earlier and jot down potential questions.
- As a member of the team, gather and organize all data, documents, log of behavior issues, intervention strategies used, and work samples ahead of time.
- Start meeting off on a positive note. Share a positive anecdote or event.
- Be sensitive to the feelings of the parents/caregivers of the child being discussed.
- Problem-solve in advance. Be ready to offer solutions or additional intervention strategies.
- Ask for support and assistance if you are unclear or do not understand the process, procedures, or forms/paperwork.
- Involve students if age appropriate. Support and encourage student-led IEP meetings. This not only allows the child to participate but also provides an opportunity to share their strengths and where they need to improve.
- Gather information and be open to learning about new resources and information.
- Be present and focused during the meeting. Have a clear mind and remain until the conclusion of the meeting. Parents/caregivers will be pleased that you are championing their child's/children's success.

Relating to parents of special needs youth is not an unreachable task. As a matter of fact, it only requires teachers and school leaders who are empathetic and humane. Parents/caregivers respond to genuine and sincere concern. Many of us have not had a special needs child to raise and educate. There are many things we take for granted. Parents of special needs children must consider the needs of their children in every setting and situation. As a result, in some instances, they may come across as unreasonable, overbearing, and demanding. Teachers and school administrators need to practice empathy, patience, and understanding.

Knowing how to relate with parents of special needs youth is just as important as knowing how to assist students and work with teachers and community stakeholders. Teachers and school administrators can turn possibly difficult or touchy situations into a win-win event for everyone. Here are several simple, down-to-earth techniques that are easy for classroom teachers and principals to utilize and implement:

- Communicate openly with the parent of special needs students prior to situations or incidents occurring. A negative incident or situation should not be the first and only contact made. Parents need to know you genuinely care about their child/children. Provide parents with updates and progress statements throughout the school year.
- Open forms of communication with something positive regardless of the situation.
- Be careful not to imply under any circumstances that their child's/children's behavior is a result of their parenting techniques.
- Use every opportunity or situation to prove information and learning for the parents. Be a resource and offer constructive ideas/techniques for them to use at home.
- Enlist their assistance and collaboration when developing behavior intervention plans.
- Diagnosing or prescribing medications is out of the purview of educators. Nor is it appropriate to share personal decisions made as a special needs parent during a meeting.
- Refrain from using labels and making jokes about a special needs child when conversing with parents/caregivers. Always use appropriate and respectful language.

- Introduce all individuals who will be working with the special needs child to the parents/caregivers. Ensure only qualified and ethical individuals are providing services.

CHAPTER 3 SUMMARY

Chapter 3 is centered on one of the main challenges parents of special needs children encounter during their educational journey. It doesn't matter what the nature of the exceptionality or extent of the disability is, gathering and securing the appropriate services and resources requires total parent engagement. I chose to focus chapter 3 on the individualized education program (IEP) because formulating and implementing the IEP document can cause serious issues if not executed with integrity. One purpose is to expand parents' current knowledge and extend their repertoire of communication skills.

This chapter also examines and discusses the role teachers and school leaders can play as IEP team members and professionals. As a result, readers of this chapter—whether a parent, classroom teacher, or school administrator—will gain tips, techniques, and strategies to ensure the educational needs are met with success. Additionally, parents and educators are provided brief examples, explanations, and tips to improve the IEP process and procedures.

The more equipped parents of special needs children are, the better they become as advocates for their children. Occasionally, parents/caregivers cross the line between advocating and demanding services. Once the line is crossed, parents endanger their relationship with the teacher and school. Whatever relationships were established earlier become strained or destroyed. Broken relationships between families and the school personnel impact the educational journey for students and their academic success. Following some of the tips, techniques, and guidelines shared will benefit students, families, and all school personnel.

4

EMPOWERING PARENTS TO NURTURE EMPOWERED YOUTH

Parent involvement and engagement research studies and reports have overwhelmingly emphasized the impact of parental involvement and engagement in schools. Parent-school-community partnerships create and enable improvement for students, teachers, parents, and communities. Strong and meaningful home-school collaborations in which parents and teachers are allies lead to a better understanding of students. With a clearer understanding of students' personalities, social skills, and peculiarities supplied by parents, teachers are better equipped to meet *specific* skill needs of students in classrooms.

This *parent* knowledge enables teachers to develop, adjust, and modify appropriate instructional experiences and activities for their students. Parental input and feedback enhance and supplement what teachers have learned about each individual student in their classroom. Additionally, students whose parents are engaged and involved in their education tend to:

- achieve more, regardless of ethnic or racial background, socioeconomic status, or parents' educational level;
- achieve better grades, test scores, and attendance;
- consistently complete their work;
- have better self-esteem and confidence;
- are more self-disciplined; and
- show higher aspirations and motivation toward school.

Although research studies have emphasized the impact and benefits of parental involvement/engagement for student achievement, there is an obvious disconnect between parents, teachers, and school administrators. Many parents do not have a clear understanding of the world of schooling and its inner workings. Generally, parents or caregivers tend to evaluate their children's schools based on their own personal past school and learning experiences. Individuals with positive past experiences are more likely to support their teachers and schools. Negative experiences result in distrust, disrespect, and lack of support.

Knowledge is power. Informed and knowledgeable parents become empowered parents. Those who have an understanding and appreciation for *schooling* can better prepare youth for future success in life. To help parents perform their role more effectively and efficiently, a simple guide designed to explain and recommend steps for them to utilize will help them navigate the transition from home to school and from school to home. A general understanding and awareness of the inner workings of schools will provide parents with a *how to* and *what to do if* parent resource guide/manual.

For parents/caregivers beginning or in the early stages of their first educational journey, the world of schooling is filled with wonder, questions, excitement, and frustrations. They use their personal experiences with learning and *schooling* as the standard for determining what schools should *be and look like*. Often these unrealistic notions/ideas serve as a cause of parental disappointments and dissatisfaction with public or private schools. Misunderstanding or different interpretations of school system policies, rules, regulations, and programs can minimize parental and community support of school leaders, teachers, and schools.

Other parents/caregivers may judge or evaluate their children's school based on past personal experiences they had as students. Parents who want more control over the curriculum and to have a say in what is taught opt to homeschool their children. Others seek charter schools or private religious schools that they feel align with their family values, beliefs, and principles. Schools wrestle continuously between meeting state/federal and system-level mandates and responding to public demands for annual high academic achievement and progress. The challenge of meeting parent and public expectations is everchanging and daunting.

Regardless of the selected educational setting or expectations for schools, a road map with resources and specific recommended strategies or suggestions would assist any parent/caregiver in providing learning experiences to aid in fostering and developing their children's full potential.

Following are my selected topics, tips, recommendations, and strategies on school-related issues or concerns to clarify and extend parents' understanding of educational organizations. This section will begin with a brief description and discussion about the role of the key person in every school: school administrator or principal. Generally, parents or caregivers are unaware of their day-to-day responsibilities. School administrators juggle many hats and possess varying levels of expertise managing and operating their staff and building.

SCHOOL ADMINISTRATORS' ROLE

Knowing and understanding a school starts with the leader of the school: the building principal. Many parents have no idea what a principal does in a school or what role he or she plays. They may see the principal standing outside greeting students during early morning arrivals and afternoon dismissals. They may know and understand that a principal is the head of the school and supervises the teachers and other staff in the building. They may also know if there is a fight on the bus or in class, violators are sent to the principal's office for a resolution. Parents, however, are not aware of principals' instructional role in their buildings.

In addition to being responsible for the overall operation of the school building, school leaders are responsible for:

- supervising, monitoring, and evaluating all faculty and staff;
- developing and writing budgets/grants;
- recruiting and hiring all staff positions;
- observing classroom instruction and providing constructive feedback;
- submitting requested system/state-level reports;
- developing the instructional, lunch, and special program schedules and services;
- maintaining the building and requesting needed repairs/updates;
- conducting stakeholder meetings for parents and concerned citizens;

- incorporating and utilizing community resources for students (e.g., Boy and Girl Scouts);
- organizing and setting up PTO/PTA and parent volunteering;
- setting up provisions/plans for parent conferences;
- scheduling professional learning opportunities for faculty and staff;
- developing and setting up a school-level leadership team;
- formulating school-wide and grade-level school improvement plans;
- adhering to school system and school-level policies and state and federal guidelines;
- meeting periodically with community and parent groups upon request;
- planning and scheduling enrichment programs and extracurricular activities and events for students;
- implementing new programs, regulations, standards, and curriculum as mandated by the superintendent and/or the state department of education;
- attending system-level administrative meetings and retreats (if instituted);
- coordinating and interpreting state assessment test results for parents and stakeholders;
- analyzing school-level test results and reports for parents and stakeholders;
- implementing and monitoring supplemental programs;
- ordering instructional supplies, equipment, and furniture; and
- annually inventory of school equipment, furniture, and Title I supplies/resources.

The above list is not all inclusive but is a good representation of many responsibilities school leaders face on a day-to-day basis. It is evident that instructional leaders are charged with the ability to manage and handle many tasks and respond professionally to their teachers, staff, teachers, parents, and other stakeholders. How do you establish a relationship with your school-level administrator? Here are some facts that parents/caregivers need to believe and accept in order to build a working relationship with their school-level administrator.

Establishing Relationships with School Administrators

Fact 1: School administrators are multitasked individuals with numerous responsibilities.

Fact 2: School administrators are people too.

Fact 3: School administrators strive to build relationships with school clientele and their stakeholders.

Fact 4: Parent, stakeholders, and community perceptions and expectations are important to school administrators.

Fact 5: School administrators value parent, stakeholder, and community feedback/input.

Recommended Guidelines for Building Relationships with School Administrators

- Show respect and understanding for the principal's time.
- Become familiar with your principal's goals for your school.
- Get to know your principal's interests and hobbies.
- Find out and follow the levels of communication and procedures for scheduling a conference.
- Jot down your questions or concerns prior to your scheduled conference with the principal.
- Allot enough time in the event a situation occurs and your meeting is interrupted.
- Be prepared to wait if you request to meet with your school administrator without an appointment.
- Stick to your point and allotted time.
- Refrain from gossiping.
- Help with rumor control.
- Show you care about your school.
- Be a good listener.
- Always conduct yourself in a positive and appropriate manner.
- Be willing to agree to disagree, if necessary.
- Become a member of the school council and school parent organizations to learn more about the school's policies, rules, and procedures.
- Read and review the school's parent handbook.

Parents/caregivers view building relationships with their child's school administrator as secondary in importance. After all, teachers have daily contact with students and really get to know them on a more personal level. Principals' contact, at best, is general in nature unless situations and circumstances require more contact and interaction. Parents need to know that school administrators do seek to build relationships with the parents of students and other stakeholders in the community. It is imperative for them to develop healthy relationships to foster cooperation and trust among their school and community clientele.

Even though the relationships between school leaders and parents are more distant, there is considerable value for them to invest in building positive relationships. According to Meador (2017), principals can build respect and trust with their constituents through meaningful relationships. Trust is not an easy value to earn. Many parents are skeptical and very distrustful of school administrators' decisions. They need to feel and know that the information shared in the administrator's office during conferences will remain with the individual. Additionally, parents need to believe principals have their child's best interests at heart.

Principals are not perfect and do make mistakes from time to time. Trust is fostered and nurtured when parents can bring issues or concerns to their school administrator and know that the situation or incident will be handled when they leave. The benefit of having parents' and stakeholders' trust gives school administrators freedom of making decisions without looking over their shoulders, worrying about possible questions, or having to defend their decision, even though parents may not always agree with or support decisions that are made.

Principals who have built trust with their parents and community are forgiven far more readily when mistakes or bad calls are made. Another benefit for principals who are intentional about building relationship with parents and stakeholders is feedback. School administrators need to get honest feedback and input from their parents and community stakeholders. The feedback received is needed to solicit information and ideas to assist in making changes and improving existing programs and initiatives. Without a strong positive relationship with their school-level administrators, parents will be reluctant to respond truthfully to questions.

There is an emphasis on schools engaging parents and community stakeholders to garner their support and buy-in as *true* partners. Forward-thinking principals utilize questionnaires to seek different ideas or thoughts on school-related issues or concerns. Parents and community stakeholders are a great source of creative and viable ideas. Well-developed questionnaires or surveys can utilize the skills and expertise of parents as an additional resource to assist with obtaining school improvement goals. On the other hand, school administrators must be willing to accept and listen to tough and honest responses received.

Inviting parents, community stakeholders, and students (if appropriate) on these committees formed to solicit feedback and input will enable participants to be a part of the inner workings of their schools. In a sense, parents and community members can be an integral part of each student's education and academic growth. Other simple strategies school administrators may utilize and implement to build meaningful relationships with parents/caregivers are:

- Spend time attending and participating in extracurricular activities and events after school or during the regular day.
- Find common ground and mutual interests among your parents and stakeholders.
- Greet and make conversations with parents, community stakeholders, and staff.
- Share personal information about your interests, hobbies, and background.
- Call five to ten parents weekly and ask them questions about the school, their child's teacher, and so on.
- Hold a parent luncheon or tea with a small group of parents/community stakeholders and talk to them about school-related issues.
- Form committees for school-related topics and invite parents/caregivers to participate.

TEACHERS' ROLE IN THE CLASSROOM

A classroom teacher's role is probably more important than a school administrator's role when it comes to your child/children. Next to their parents and other significant family members, teachers are second in importance in a child's life. Teachers influence and impact children's learning, intellectual growth, overall well-being, and future. Therefore, it is imperative that all parents make a concerted effort to build a positive relationship with their child's classroom teachers. Teachers are powerful and knowledgeable allies for parents/caregivers. They see and interact with your child/children in a different setting—the classroom.

Teachers provide information and feedback that help parents/caregivers work effectively with their child(ren) at home. A strong positive partnership between a teacher and a child's parent(s) creates an impenetrable fortress of support, encouragement, and motivation. Additionally, positive relationships with classroom teachers affect children's success in school, which impacts children at any age. Benefits associated with positive parent-teacher relationships are social confidence, motivation, and academic achievement. Developing a positive relationship is a shared venture nurtured over time between the parent and teacher.

Occasionally, parents may have difficulty building a relationship with their child's teacher. When faced with a situation of this nature, school administrators strive to resolve the issue, if possible. Difficulties can arise between a teacher and parent as a result of a difference of opinion about grades, an assignment, discipline, educational philosophies, classroom procedures, or homework policy. Sometimes it's a matter of personality differences between the parent and the child. What's important is the child and his/her feelings about what is going on around him/her. It is always crucial that the parent and teacher remain professional.

Reinke (2016) strongly recommends that parents or caregivers who find themselves not liking or caring for their child's/children's teacher should:

- *Keep their anger in check.* Children should not hear you vent or see your frustration. Take time to cool off and refrain from saying anything negative about the teacher with the child present. This may damage the relationship children already have with their teacher. It puts them in an awkward situation and may cause them to behave disrespectfully toward the teacher.
- *Take action.* Be proactive. Don't wait for things to fester and grow worse. As soon as you have a problem with a teacher, schedule a meeting as soon as possible. If you don't feel comfortable meeting with the teacher, schedule a meet with the principal and be specific about what the issue or concern is. Be willing to compromise, if necessary.

- *Observe.* If you are not certain what the problem is or what is causing your child's difficulty, volunteer in the classroom and attend classroom events. Be objective when observing. Spending time in the classroom will help you determine the dynamics between the teacher and your child.

The goal of parents and teachers should be to keep the children motivated. If there are differences of opinion and they are handled in a professional manner, children can learn what to do and how to conduct themselves when there are differences. The parent and teacher must keep the line of communication open. Children will possibly face similar challenges in their future. With proper actions by the adults, children will learn how to recognize and resolve conflicts in the future. It is the responsibility of parents to be a positive role model.

Establishing Relationships with Teachers

Fact 1: Teachers are human beings with interests and hobbies.

Fact 2: Teachers have varying skill levels, expertise, and personalities.

Fact 3: Teachers seek support, cooperation, collaboration, and partnering with parents.

Fact 4: Teachers want all students to learn, grow, and succeed.

Fact 5: Teachers strive to build relationships and connect with students and parents.

Fact 6: Teachers want to know they are respected and appreciated.

Listed below are several recommended tips to help parents/caregivers start the school year off building a positive relationship with classroom teachers. Note: This list is not all inclusive.

Recommended Tips for Building a Positive Relationship with Teachers

- *Meet with the teacher(s) and staff.* Make a concerted effort to meet the school-level principal and office staff too.

- *Find out how the teacher wants to be reached in the event of an emergency, question, and/or concern.* Keep your contact information up to date and notify the teacher of any changes as soon as possible.
- *Be respectful of the teacher's time.* Report on time for meetings and conferences. Schedule meetings that are convenient for you and your child's teacher. Refrain from showing up at the classroom door to conference with the teacher at inappropriate times of the day.
- *Never talk negatively about your child's teacher in front of your child.* Be a role model for your child and always display a good example of appropriate behavior.
- *Say "Thank you."* Express your appreciation for big and little things. Cards, thank you notes, and small gifts can go a long way with teachers and other school personnel.
- *Show up for special events.* Show your support by attending different classroom and school functions or activities. Volunteer, go on field trips, attend parent meetings, if you are available.
- *Spread the word.* If your child's teacher is doing something special with the class or has done something unique for your child, share the news with your teacher's principal. Teachers often hang onto notes or letters written by parents and students expressing their thanks and appreciation.

Building a positive relationship with your child's school administrator, teacher, and other school personnel is the first step in starting off on the right foot as you begin your educational journey. The simplest way to establish relationships with your child's teacher and school's principal is to simply schedule a meeting to get to know them. Teachers and principals are people-oriented and love communicating with parents and other stakeholders to share information about their students (parents only), school's programs, and goals. Parents can also get to know their teachers and principals through a variety of school-related activities.

Meeting with parents, community stakeholders, and concerned citizens enables them to enlist the support and buy-in needed for school projects, parent-community partnerships, school events, and school improvement initiatives. From time to time, there are situations that arise that require the attention of school administrators and teachers. Life does happen and like any other organization or workplace, schools too are often challenged with people situations, issues, or problems that demand their immediate attention. The threat of an abduction attempt or the appearance of a social worker are examples of issues needing immediate attention.

What do you do if you have a pressing or urgent situation and the teacher or principal is not available? Do you demand their immediate presence and attention on the spot? Or do you contact the superintendent's office since you were unable to meet with either individual requested? Most schools have an administrative team and a formal line of communication that school administrators use to respond to issues, concerns, needs, and requests from parents and other stakeholders. Parents can lessen or eliminate frustration and confusion by adhering to outlined steps.

Specific procedures are usually posted on school system websites or written in parent/student handbooks. If you have any questions or want additional clarification about the procedure or guidelines, contact the appropriate school-level contact person. A good place to begin is with your child's/children's classroom teacher. In the event the school administrator and teacher are unavailable/absent, the suggestions below are reasonable and appropriate for any serious matter or situation.

Recommended Guidelines and Protocol

- Be calm, professional, and in control of your emotions.
- Ask to whom you can speak to share confidential or urgent information in place of the principal or teacher. The individual suggested may be the assistant principal, a school counselor, or a designee.
- Non-time-sensitive or extremely critical information can be put in writing and placed in a sealed envelope for the principal or teacher. Note on the envelope *Urgent* (if applicable). Request a copy of the letter for your file. Remember to include up-to-date contact information and a specific contact, if needed.
- Allow at least twenty-four hours for a response from the principal or teacher. Note: If the information requires a response deadline, indicate the time in the letter for the principal/teacher. You may also write on the outside of the envelope *Need a response by* _____.

LEVELS OF COMMUNICATION

Like businesses, major corporations, companies, and other organizations, all schools have a network of communication for employees and the public to follow to address issues, concerns, questions, complaints, and recommendations. Established networks of communication direct clients and consumers to the appropriate departments and/or individuals who can answer specific questions or who are responsible for designated areas/ topics. Most schools have classroom teachers as the first level of communication if parents have concerns or questions about classroom procedures, discipline, instruction, curriculum, and so forth.

Generally, teachers are very appreciative when parents direct their questions or concerns to them first before contacting the principal or assistant principal. Some teachers view not speaking or meeting with them first about an issue or concern as going over their heads. They want the opportunity to address and resolve the issue before it is referred to their school administrator. Once teachers feel overlooked and not respected as a professional, it is hard to maintain a positive parent-teacher relationship for the remainder of the school year. They'll feel undermined and not supported and dread future encounters or interactions with the parent(s)/caregiver(s).

Recommended Guidelines and Protocol

- Communicate/meet with the individual as a first step whenever there's a concern or issue.
- Direct any classroom-related concerns, issues, or questions to teachers first.
- If the teacher is absent or unavailable, contact the school counselor/ principal to share your concern, issue, or question. Ask the school counselor/principal to share your concern with the teacher and request a conference.
- All urgent matters or situations should be directed to the administrative team.
- If you have spoken or met with the classroom teacher and are not satisfied with the response, move to the next level of communication: assistant principal or principal. Be sure to let the administrator know you have spoken to the classroom teacher and you're not satisfied.

Also indicate what plan or solution was implemented to resolve the issue or concern. Providing this information will let the principal/assistant principal know the prior plan of action. Dissatisfaction or continuing issues after meeting with an assistant principal or school counselor should be reported to the school administrator.

- Always maintain your professionalism, emotional control, and objectivity.
- Disagreements with a school administrator's decision/resolution should be discussed with the appropriate central office–level administrator. Check your school system's staff directory or with central office staff to find out the appropriate person to contact.
- The superintendent is the highest level of communication if the issue or concern has not been resolved satisfactorily after going through the prior levels. The goal is to come to a resolution that represents a win-win situation for all parties involved.

CHAPTER 4 SUMMARY

In order to effectively empower parents/caregivers, we must equip them with the proper tools. One of the most important tools needed is knowledge. Chapter 4 explored, examined, and shared several topics to explain and clarify the roles of school administrators and classroom teachers. The author provided parents with tips and recommendations to help them establish positive relationships with their children's teachers and school administrators. Building and establishing relationships is key for ensuring academic success and well-being for all children.

Chapter 4 also describes briefly the roles of school administrators and teachers, so parents and community stakeholders will gain a better understanding of what principals do on a day-to-day basis. It is hoped that this updated information will foster a greater appreciation and knowledge of challenges school administrators face.

Building positive relationships is a key factor for the success of all children/youth. Parents and teachers play major parts in guaranteeing academic success in classrooms. Listed are recommended strategies for parents, teachers, and school administrators to use to foster and nurture strong positive relationships among each other. Although the relationship between parents and teachers is imperative, school administrators need to build relationships with parents and the community to develop trust and gain respect. Feedback and input principals receive from their parents and community stakeholders strengthen support and buy-in.

5

DEMYSTIFYING SCHOOLING

For parents/caregivers beginning their first experience with public schools, the first day of school is exciting and filled with expectations. It has finally arrived! Little Johnny or Susie is starting preschool or kindergarten and have prepared all summer long for this day. Some parents face that first day with anticipation and wonder. Others see the first day of school as their babies leaving the safety and security of home. Many breathe a sigh of relief and use this significant event as a step toward more freedom or other opportunities. Whatever the reasons or emotions, everyone has preconceived expectations for and ideas about school.

Sometimes past negative experiences and preconceived ideas about school become the source of disillusionments, disappointments, and dissatisfaction among new and/or transferring parents. When you add feelings of discontent into the mix, it makes readily accepting and following new rules, procedures, and policies of schools a hard pill to swallow. If parents/caregivers start the school year off in this state of mind, there is almost no hope for building strong positive relationships with their child's teachers, school administrator, or school. Unhappy parents/caregivers lead to unhappy and unsuccessful children.

An integral part of empowering parents/caregivers is increasing their knowledge base and understanding about schools. Before beginning this journey of unlocking and clarifying what makes up *schooling*, parents must accept a few basic facts that are germane to all schools whatever the educational setting may be—public, private, religious, or homeschool. They are:

- All schools are governed/guided by a rule-making/policymaking board or organization.
- All schools need rules, policies, and procedures to operate efficiently and effectively.
- All schools develop/implement guidelines and standards for the overall safety, health, and well-being of students.
- All schools have curriculum designed to address the intellectual development of all students' needs.
- All schools have high expectations for their students.
- All schools have regulations and funding resources.
- All schools have a philosophy of learning for their students.
- All schools make a commitment to professional development for faculty and staff.

Note: The above listing is author selected and not all inclusive. Following are brief explanations of selected common rules, procedures, and practices parents/caregivers may encounter in schools. It is hoped that these explanations and rationales will prepare parents for the reality of schooling and help them adjust a little easier to the school environment.

SCHOOL RULES, PROCEDURES, POLICIES, AND REGULATIONS

There isn't any organization, workplace, trade, profession, or institution that doesn't have rules, procedures, regulations, and policies to govern their existence or operation. Policymaking, certifying, and licensing bodies set standards/guideline to ensure quality. Schools operate like other organizations and are expected to follow federal, state, Department of Education, and school system policies and guidelines. Without rules, regulations, procedures, and policies, schools would be chaotic and nonproductive. Much like schools, parents too have rules, procedures, and principles to maintain a functioning and safe environment to rear children.

Fact 1: Policies, rules, regulations, and procedures are necessary and needed.
Fact 2: Many policies, rules, regulations, and procedures are mandated by state departments of education, the school system's board of education, and federal/state mandates.

Fact 3: There is a rationale for every rule, policy, regulation, and procedure implemented.

Fact 4: School Administrators implement regulations, rules, policies, and procedures to meet specific needs of their building and staff. Note: Parents often can provide input or feedback to improve or adjust, if needed.

Recommended Guidelines and Protocol for Parents/Caregivers

- Read and review organizations' policies, rules, and regulations, usually located on their website or in school handbooks.
- Direct questions or concerns to the appropriate-level individual.
- Attend school- and system-level council meetings for parents and other stakeholders to gain additional information and understanding.
- Schedule a meeting with the school administrator if you have any questions or concerns about school procedures, policies, and rules.

Opening School Exercise: Recitation of the Pledge of Allegiance

Schools generally begin the instructional day with school staff and children reciting the Pledge of Allegiance. If for some reason you don't want your child/children to participate in this opening exercise, let teachers know as soon as possible. Also, it's an excellent idea to review this information in your school's parent/student handbook or on their website *before* the first day of school. This will eliminate unnecessary misunderstandings for the classroom teacher and student. School systems have policies with written alternatives for children. Many schools ask students to recite a school pledge or slogan after reciting the pledge.

THE ROLE OF PARENT TEACHER ASSOCIATIONS OR PARENT TEACHER ORGANIZATIONS

Getting parents involved with their child's/children's school is a way to gain support and connect the home and school. PTAs and PTOs exist to help parents and teachers collaborate and work together to do what's best for the children and the school. Joining your school's parent teacher association or parent teacher organization is an excellent way to learn more about your school and develop relations with teachers and other school clientele. Many of these organizations offer learning sessions for parents and conduct fundraising activities or events to support and augment school's instructional programs.

> *Fact 1:* Parent organizations, whether public, private, or homeschool, focus on school, teacher, student, and parent needs.
> *Fact 2:* Parent teacher organizations have national/state standards, principles, and guidelines.
> *Fact 3:* Parent teacher organizations' goals may vary from organization to organization.
> *Fact 4:* Parent teacher organizations essentially consist of parent volunteering, encouraging teachers and students, promoting the welfare of students and families, and community involvement.

Recommended Guidelines and Protocol for Parents/Caregivers

- Contact your school's parent teacher organization for information about membership, goals, and activities.
- Direct all school-related questions or concerns to the classroom teacher or administrative team members.
- Attend orientations offered for volunteering in classrooms or school prior to volunteering. Follow all expressed or written volunteer guidelines shared.
- Always conduct yourself in a professional manner.
- Be willing to share your skills and expertise with your school and child's/children's classroom teacher.
- Dress appropriately.
- Refrain from disciplining students. Report inappropriate behaviors or incidents to school personnel.
- Be willing to serve your school wherever needed.
- Be accepting and understanding of the school's diverse student body and staff.
- Interact positively with teachers, staff, students, and parents.
- Be consistent as a volunteer and contact the school if emergencies arise.
- Be an ambassador for your school.

OFFICE PROCEDURES FOR PARENTS, VISITORS, AND OUTSIDE STAKEHOLDERS

Schools have a challenging task and responsibility to ensure the safety and well-being of their students and staff in the building. To perform this responsibility, specific guidelines are established for the welfare of all. Occasionally, parents as well as visitors perceive these procedures as demeaning, time consuming, nonessential, and encroaching on their rights as taxpaying citizens.

Security equipment and other safety measures have been implemented to help schools meet the challenge of providing secure, safe, and nurturing learning environments.

Schools often have other procedures in place to further help ensure safety for students and school clientele in the building. Sometimes what seems to be tedious, repetitive, unnecessary, or nonsensible is needed and prevalent in many schools.

Unknowing and misunderstanding parents and stakeholders will challenge the safety procedures and policies, causing conflicts. Brief examples are presented to dispel misunderstandings and clarify the purpose of these school procedures or guidelines.

- *Displaying Photo ID to Pick Up, Sign Out, or Visit the School/ Classroom:* Requesting a photo ID is necessary and must be enforced regardless of how many times you visit the school or check out/sign in your child/children. Make sure you always have an ID on your person.
- *Name Tag and/or Visitor's Badge:* Schools need to know who is in the building and their location. Wear your name tag and/or visitor's badge until you leave the building. Also, remain in the classroom or where you have been approved to be. Do not roam building/halls or *drop in* to say hello to your child/children or visit a former teacher. It is very important not to interrupt instruction in classrooms. You can assist schools by reporting to the office staff immediately anyone you see without a badge or name tag.
- *Escorting/Walking Children to Classrooms:* Schools monitor and supervise movement in halls throughout the school day. Some schools have specific times parents may walk their child/children to

classrooms in the morning. Check to see what procedures are established for the school your children attend.

- *Early Pickups:* Occasionally parents may have an emergency, a change in how a child goes home, or a different person signing out the child/children. All individuals who are authorized to pick up your child need to be added to the file for your child/children. Also, let the individual know that he/she must present a photo ID even though they have been added to your list.

- *Transportation and Pickup Alterations:* Changes in how a child goes home or who is picking them up need to be shared with the office staff as soon as possible. Contact the school early to allow them time to confirm the change by contacting you. *Note: Schools vary in how they handle this procedure.* They may not call to confirm the change. Make sure your child/children are aware of any changes made. Let them know who to expect too. They begin to wonder or think something has happened to you. Children become anxious and upset when they have to do something different without being notified.

- *Arrival and Departure:* Schools designate specific times to begin and end the instructional day. Selected school staff are assigned to halls and different areas of the building to supervise/monitor children during early morning arrival and dismissal times. Adhere to the times outlined by your school. Refrain from sending children to school too early and picking them up late. Staff are usually not available before the designated start time and after dismissal to monitor/supervise children.

- *School Traffic Pattern Plan:* To ensure safe arrivals and dismissals for students who are transported by cars or buses, school administrators develop a traffic plan that will work best for all students whether they walk or ride to school. These plans are sent home and/ or posted on schools' websites. If you see any potential safety hazards or issues, report them immediately to the office.

- *Authorized Searches:* School administrators and the administrative team have the authority to search book bags if there is just cause. Students do bring items to school in book bags or on the school bus or have items on their person that are inappropriate for school. Periodically check your child/children's book bag. Be assured that searches only occur when there is just cause or reasonable suspicion. Your child/children's rights are not being violated during an authorized search.

- *Scheduling Teacher Conferences:* Most schools require parents to formally request and schedule a conference with their child's/children's teacher(s). Teachers welcome contact with parents and will set aside time to have a conference to share students' growth, academic progress, concerns, or issues. In some instances, schools designate specific day(s) throughout the school year for parent-teacher conferences. These special days are held during the day (early dismissal of students) or in the evening. Follow the procedure established in your school system. Refrain from conducting *on-the-spot* conferences.

- *Classroom Observations:* Observing your child during classroom instruction is a way to see how your child performs during instructional time as well as gain an understanding of classroom expectations. Classroom observations, like parent conferences, should be scheduled. Check with the office staff to find out if there are specific guidelines for this activity. Know children usually behave differently when their parent is in the classroom. Make special arrangements with the teacher and school administrator to observe your child without being in the classroom.

- *Birthday and Special Celebrations:* The most joyous day for children can be the most frustrating day for parents. Schools have different procedures for handling birthday celebrations during the instructional day. Don't assume you can send *Happy Birthday* balloons to the classroom or have a birthday party during lunchtime. Some schools allow store-bought cupcakes and the singing of "Happy Birthday" during lunch. Be mindful of children who have food allergies. Confer with your school's office and teacher before planning a birthday surprise.

- *Birthday Party Invitations (Private):* Teachers and schools may have guidelines for distributing invitations to private birthday parties in school. Teachers are always mindful of the emotional and social well-being of all students in their class/building. Feelings are often hurt when only selected students receive invitations and others are not included. Before you instruct your child/children to distribute invitations to selected classmates, check to see if there are specific guidelines first.

- *Valentine's Day:* Children love exchanging cards with their classmates. Schools are not permitted to share addresses or contact information of classmates due to privacy and security. However, teachers do send home names (first names only) of children in the classroom. If your school has specific guidelines for this special day, follow what is outlined. If there isn't anything in your school's handbook, check with the classroom teacher for information and instructions. If Valentine's Day cards are exchanged during the school day, send enough cards for each student in the classroom.
- *Medications:* Children should not be sent to school with medication on their person. Generally, schools have policies regarding medication and other health-related concerns. Many schools have licensed LPNs (licensed practical nurses) or RNs (registered nurses) on their staff full or part time to handle, oversee, and monitor the health needs of students. Schools without certified health officials train office personnel to handle the health needs of students and staff. Review your system's or school's policies about the administration of medication.
- *Dress Codes:* What is acceptable for students as well as staff to wear to school varies by states and regions. This is another area that might be frustrating and cause conflicts and disputes. More issues surface as children transition to middle and high school. It is wise and cost effective to find out what is deemed appropriate by your school/system. Additionally, there may be restrictions regarding footwear and lengths of shirts, dresses, skirts, and blouses (and also their transparency). Older students start to experiment and push boundaries testing their independence and strong desire to impress peers.
- *School Parties:* Schools have schoolwide parties and individual classroom celebrations for special days or holidays (Christmas/Easter). Generally, schools will list parties that are held during the school year. If for religious or personal reasons you don't want your child/children to participate, inform the teacher(s) so other arrangements can be made. Some parents choose to keep their child/children at home. Know keeping your child/children home due to a class or schoolwide party or event is not an excused absence. *Note: Absence due to religious beliefs is acceptable with relevant documentation.*

- *Field Trips:* Teacher supplement classroom instruction and broaden the experiences of students through real-life experiences. Field trips can range from walking trips to a local fire station to a visit to a museum. Parental permission is required for students to participate in all field trips. Parents are often asked to accompany classes to help monitor/supervise students. Depending on your school's or school system's policy, parent chaperones may or may not be able to accompany the children on the school bus. In some cases, you may have to follow the bus in your car to the field trip site. Adhere to all procedures outlined.
- *Siblings' Attendance at School Events:* There will be schoolwide events that lend themselves to participation by younger and older siblings and friends such as festivals, sports, family nights, spring flings, concerts, art shows, plays, and talent shows. There will be, however, class activities or events that do not lend themselves to participation of younger siblings. For example, if you are volunteering in a classroom or helping with a class Valentine's Day party, arrangements should be made for younger siblings and/or friends.
- *Discipline and Student Code of Conduct:* Student code of conduct and discipline are two very important areas for parents. Read and review the policies indicated carefully and share them with your child/children. Direct any questions to the school administrator or assistant principal.
- *Homework Policy:* Policies about homework vary from school system to school system and school to school. Teachers usually assign homework to provide additional practice and maintain and reinforce concepts/skills currently or previously taught. Additionally, teachers consider the grade level and specific student/class needs when determining the length of assignments. Struggles with homework that require you to *instruct* your child/children are an indication of nonmastery or understanding of the skill/concept taught. Contact your child's/children's teachers immediately about the situation.

Recommended Guidelines and Protocol for Parents/Caregivers

- Designate a specific place or area for homework.

- Briefly review the directions or instructions with your child/children before they work on their own.
- Encourage your child/children to explain their assignment to check their understanding.
- Periodically check and monitor their progress on the assignment.
- Report visible signs of difficulty or expressed concerns to your child's/children's teacher.
- Designate a distraction-free area/space for your child/children to complete their homework.
- Utilize older siblings to assist younger siblings. Ensure siblings understand they aren't to do their homework for them.
- Contact the teacher to make sure you are explaining homework using the appropriate terminology and process.

- *Inclement Weather and Emergency Procedures:* Bad weather and emergency procedures are generally available in the school-level parent handbook. Additionally, school districts contact parents direct through e-mail blasts and telephone calls. School closings or other emergency situations are broadcast via radio and television. Be aware of your school's special procedures for emergencies. If you have questions about the process, direct them immediately to the office. Don't wait for an emergency or bad weather situation to occur. Also, as a parent, you need to establish a plan for your child/children if dismissal times are altered.
- *School System Calendar:* School calendars are very informative and need to be followed and checked periodically. Avoid scheduling doctor's appointments for your children on important test and assessment dates. Also, refrain from having your child/children miss school to be in weddings, go house hunting, or go on vacations to Disney World. There are, however, times or circumstances when absences are unavoidable.
- *Fire and Intruder Drills:* Schools have specific procedures in place for monthly unannounced drills for students and their staff. It is very important that everyone knows what to do, where to go, and how to exit the building, if necessary. Intruder drill procedures are not shared with parents.

CLASSROOM ASSIGNMENTS AND TEACHER SELECTION

Veteran and new parents often struggle with developing positive relationships with teachers and communicating effectively when there are issues or concerns. Understanding what takes place in classrooms is an area that can be challenging and a source of confusion and conflicts. Parents have different ideas of the type of teacher they want for their child/children. They also have different ideas on the skills or qualities the *ideal* teacher should possess. Parents base their teacher expectations on personal experiences and comments from other parents or determine a teacher's *fit* for their child's/children's happiness in the classroom.

No matter what process is used by schools to set up classrooms for the school year, there always are parents who request a different teacher for a variety of reasons. Occasionally moves or changes are made for the best interest of both parties involved. School administrators have several variables to consider when setting up classes such as ethnicity, number of retainees, special needs students, gender ratio, and class enrollment numbers. *Note: This is not all inclusive. Other variables may be considered when setting up classes.* Some schools have procedures in place that allow parents to have input on selecting classroom teachers.

Fact 1: Teachers vary in their skill and expertise levels.

Fact 2: Teachers are people too.

Fact 3: Teachers have different instructional styles and classroom procedures.

Fact 4: Teachers are required to update their certification.

Fact 5: Teachers are evaluated annually to assess instructional effectiveness.

Fact 6: Teachers seek to establish positive relationships with students and parents.

Recommended Guidelines and Protocol for Parents/Caregivers

- Refrain from seeking information about teachers from neighbors or friends.
- Schedule meetings with teachers as soon as a question, concern, or issue arises.
- Don't compare your child's/children's teachers with other teachers.

- Remember teachers have different personalities. Try to develop a relationship with your child's/children's teachers.
- Keep your communication with teachers positive and professional.
- Share any situations or changes that may affect your child/children with the teacher.
- Consult your child's/children's teacher if you have questions about classroom procedures, behavior expectations, class rules, grades, homework, standards, and curriculum.
- Provide teachers with up-to-date contact information.
- Inform teachers of your preferred method of contact.
- Always attend conferences as scheduled.
- Enlist the help of an advocate if you are unsure of what questions to ask or need additional support during special education meetings and other conferences.
- Take advantage of classroom volunteer activities, if applicable, that fit your schedule.
- Review classroom rules and behavior expectations with your child/children periodically throughout the school year.
- Avoid criticizing and speaking negatively about teachers and school staff in the presence of your child/children.
- Sign and return in a timely manner forms and papers sent home for parent signature.
- Check your child's/children's book bag/backpack daily for communication from teachers, PTAs/PTOs, and the school.
- Classroom rules are implemented in classrooms to assist in maintaining appropriate behavior to enhance and protect instructional time. Many teachers develop classroom rules with the input of their students. Students who follow classroom rules and self-regulate their behavior may earn rewards (no homework pass, extra recess time, library pass, etc.) depending on the plan established by the classroom teacher or grade-level team.

BEHAVIOR MANAGEMENT—WHEN THE WORLD IS IN TURMOIL

All parents have probably experienced receiving a phone call from school from time to time. A sick child is something that is easier to handle and deal with. A child misbehaving in the classroom, fighting on the playground, or name calling is not. Just when you felt everything was going along smoothly, your presence now is being requested by the classroom teacher, assistant principal, or principal. What steps should be taken if your child expresses having problems at school? What next steps should be considered if children state not liking school or their teachers? Are there signs that indicate a need for attention?

According to Fuller (1999), children needing additional attention display the following characteristics that should be handled immediately by teachers and parents to avoid impacting the learning process:

1. has nightmares or sleepwalks;
2. is sick in the mornings (may develop stomachaches, headaches, or other symptoms on school days);
3. shows anxiety and nervousness;
4. has a loss of appetite;
5. clings to parent in the morning and begs not to go to school;
6. develops a fear of a specific person or situation;
7. lacks self-confidence;
8. always asks for help without attempting to do things on his/her own;
9. needs lots of praise and reassurance;
10. makes excuses for not working in class or not turning in homework;
11. is constantly dropping things, daydreaming, and leaving work unfinished;
12. withdraws from learning or stops trying;
13. is depressed (which in younger children may be expressed by aggressive, irritating behavior and in older children by sadness and fatigue); or
14. is a late bloomer or delayed developmentally.

Fact 1: Things can happen anytime and any day.
Fact 2: No one is perfect. Adults and children make mistakes.
Fact 3: Children also learn from poor choices made.
Fact 4: Receiving calls from school due to misbehavior is not the end of the world.

Fact 5: Children will make fewer poor choices as they develop and strengthen self-regulation of their behavior.

Fact 6: Some children may experience adjustment issues with school and teachers.

Fact 7: Be an advocate for your children in all situations or incidents.

Fact 8: Initiate contact as soon as a problem or situation is noted.

Recommended Guidelines and Protocol for Parents/Caregivers

- Schedule a conference or meet with the school officials as soon as possible.
- Discuss the incident with your child/children and obtain their version of what happened.
- Do not pass judgment and listen with an open mind.
- Gather information and facts about the situation or incident.
- Support the action plan and resolution accepted collaboratively between parties involved.
- Include your child/children in the conference, if it's feasible.
- Encourage your child/children to problem solve and develop a plan of action if faced with a similar situation in the future.
- Follow-up at home should be age appropriate with a consequence that aligns with the incident.
- Focus on what is best for the child/children involved.
- Be objective and open to different perspectives of a situation or incident.
- Be willing to agree to disagree and voice your opinion in a professional manner.
- Be quick to forgive and slow to condemn.
- Allow your child /children to accept responsibility for their actions.

It is difficult for a parent to accept the fact that his/her child is a behavior problem or is having other difficulties learning in the classroom. Everyone wants their children to excel and be successful in school. There is never any one single cause why a child may have difficulty in school. On some occasions, a change in a teacher or classroom may resolve some of the issues. Whatever the cause of a child's difficulty with learning or school, parents and teachers working as a collaborative team can provide support and help the child learn and grow through difficult times.

According to Sledge (2017), parents' expectations for their children to excel in academic and other areas may cause children to behave inappropriately when they are not meeting their parents' expectation. She strongly suggests that parents need to help their children feel self-empowered to improve and promote good behavior. Sledge states a great start for combatting the onset of inappropriate behavior is parents reexamining their expectations for children. With realistic expectations, parents can encourage the development of self-empowerment and good behavior in their children.

Below are recommended tips to help encourage children's self-empowerment and good behavior:

1. *Encouragement:* Put courage and/or belief in your child. Encourage them to see themselves as they are. Remember words are powerful, and children are like sponges; they soak up everything you say or do. Your words of criticism just like encouragements can have a major impact on children. Consider the words you use and choose them carefully.

2. *Mirroring:* Serve as the reflection of your child's ability, behavior, skills, and qualities. Allow them to see themselves as they truly are. Always highlight their accomplishments., strengths, and abilities. While giving them a compliment such as "Sarah, you are so creative; I love your artwork," become aware of their reaction (facial expression: smiles or physical reaction: hugs).

3. *Highlight Their Drive/Determination:* Compliment their hard work, positive behavior, and achievements. Acknowledge within yourself and to your child that they are doing their best. Remember highlighting their display of achievements whether big or small is monumental for your child's development. It's okay to pinpoint things they need to work on, but how you deliver your message is just as important as the message itself. Giving constructive criticism while emphasizing the use of positive feedback is essential.

4. *Teach with Positive Reinforcements:* Rewarding with praise often leads to more positive behavior and increases positive self-esteem. Pinpointing negative behavior can reduce negative behavior, but it does not increase positive behavior. Teach and reward your child through action and words.

5. *Power of Uniqueness:* Start at a young age. Ingrain in your child the importance of their authentic self. Encourage them to take pride in their greatest assets and individuality. Continuous use of encouragement throughout their lifespan allows your child to easily accept changes, know how to appropriately deal with challenges, and self-regulate their emotions more easily.

CONFERENCING WITH TEACHERS

Many parents, for a variety of reasons, are uncomfortable dealing with school personnel as well as their child's/children's teachers. These feelings of discomfort may be tied to past relationships or unpleasant experiences with schools. Some parents have been scarred by ineffective teachers and struggles they had during their own academic journeys. Others may be limited by their inability to speak and understand English. Still others view schools as bureaucratic organizations with meaningless rules, procedures, and policies. Whether or not parents choose a public, private, charter, or homeschool educational setting, conferences are needed.

Other areas of concern and uncertainty for parents are knowing what questions to ask about their child/children and understanding the information being shared during the conference. Uncertainty makes parents feel apprehensive, anxious, and intimidated. They don't realize that they are a very important part of an effective parent-teacher conference. Conferences should be free of educational jargon and readily understandable. Parents should feel comfortable enough to ask questions or ask for additional clarification, if needed. Interpreters for non-English speakers should be available also.

Fact 1: Teachers utilize conferences to inform parents of their child's/ children's progress.

Fact 2: Teacher conferences can be used to build relationships and improve the home-school connection.

Fact 3: Parents' contributions as active participants are needed and valued.

Fact 4: Teachers receive training on conducting effective parent conferences.

Fact 5: Teachers are encouraged to develop and build positive relationships with parents.

Fact 6: Parent-teacher conferences allow an exchange of perspectives, perceptions, and information.

Fact 7: Parents' knowledge and insights about their children help teachers develop/prepare appropriate learning activities and classroom instruction for their students.

Fact 8: Teachers want what is best for their students and are willing to try *out-of-the-box* strategies or techniques.

Recommended Guidelines and Protocol for Parents/Caregivers

- Be on time and attend all conferences scheduled. If an emergency occurs, contact the office or teacher as soon as possible to reschedule.
- Be open to conferences via telephone or other available technological communication.
- Write down any questions you have ahead of time. Beginning your conference with specific questions will help you focus on what is important regarding your child/children.
- Prepare for the upcoming conference by talking with your child to see if he/she has any questions to ask the teacher. Also, ask your child if there is anything the teacher will bring up during the conference that you need to know before the meeting. Write down your child's/children's responses to questions asked. Also, write your thoughts in response to your child's thoughts or questions.
- Share with the teacher any observations you have noted about how your child learns at home.
- Do not compare your child's/children's progress or growth with younger or older siblings or friends.
- If you have a concern, start the conference with a positive comment first.
- Keep your conference friendly and positive.
- Be solution oriented.

Listed below are questions recommended for parents to ask teachers during their child's/children's teacher conference.

1. What academic standards do you use and what do I need to know about them?
2. How will you respond if or when my child struggles in class?

3. What is the most important complex (content-related) ideas my child needs to understand by the end of the year?
4. Do you focus on strengths, weaknesses, or both?
5. How are creativity and innovative thinking used daily in your classroom?
6. How is critical thinking used daily in your classroom?
7. How are assessments designed to promote learning rather than simple measurement?
8. What can I do to support literacy in my home?
9. What kinds of questions do you suggest that I ask my children daily about your class?
10. How exactly is learning personalized in your classroom? In your school?
11. How do you measure academic progress and growth?
12. What are the most common instructional or literacy strategies you will use this school year?
13. What learning models do you use (e.g., project-based learning, mobile learning, game-based learning), and what do you see as the primary benefits of that approach?
14. What are the best school or district resources that we should consider using as a family to support our child in the classroom?
15. Is there technology you'd recommend that can help support my child in self-directed learning?
16. What are the most common barriers you see to academic progress in your classroom?
17. How is education changing?
18. How do you see the role of the teacher in the learning process?
19. What am I not asking but should be?
20. How is my child doing socially?
21. What do you see as my child's strengths and/or weaknesses?
22. What do you think are academic challenges for my child?
23. Name the five top skills you hope your students will walk away with at the end of the school year.
24. How do you best prefer to communicate with me?
25. Is my child on grade level for reading? What about math, science, and writing?

26. How do you support children in their social development? For example, how do you address challenges that happen at recess, lunch, or PE?

27. How does the school handle standardized testing and preparation for tests?

28. Can we talk more about your homework policy and how my child is doing with homework?

29. What can I do at home to support what you are doing in the classroom?

30. Who does my child work well with?

31. Does my child ask questions or request help if he/she doesn't understand or is having trouble?

32. Does my child contribute to class discussions?

33. Does my child make friends easily?

34. Is my child able to self-regulate his/her behavior?

35. Are there behaviors you are seeing at school (both good and bad) that you think I might not see at home?

36. Is my child a learner during recess?

37. Does my child seem to be happy during the instructional day?

38. What can we do at home to promote growth in a fun and stimulating way?

39. Are there any field trips and is there a cost to families?

40. What is your policy on late homework and make-up work?

41. What can I do if my child gets stuck on homework at home?

42. How do you handle absences and missed tests, assignments, or homework?

43. How can I help my child be more organized with homework without taking it over completely?

44. Is my child giving and showing his/her best effort?

45. What will have the biggest impact on my child's grades this year?

46. Does my child have too many extracurricular activities from your vantage point?

47. What is your teaching style and how can we be consistent with your method at home?

48. What are your suggestions for limiting online time and social media at home?

49. How can I best stay on top of what is happening in the classroom? In school?

50. What can I do to support you to make your job easier as we work as a team for my child's growth this year?

BEING AT ODDS

It is not unusual for parents and teachers to have different opinions and perceptions of what is best for children. There isn't a principal who hasn't had to solve issues or concerns that may arise as the result of a teacher's instructional practice or discipline decision. In many instances, these situations are resolved after a brief explanation or clarification. There are, however, circumstances that warrant more time and patience for a resolution that will work for all parties involved. The focus of a conference under this circumstance should be to maintain a positive relationship in order to support the child's learning and academic progress.

Key to maintaining a positive relationship between a parent and a teacher is a school leader's ability to handle a situation before a parent-teacher's relationship is destroyed. Once the teacher-parent partnership deteriorates, the educational well-being of the child in the classroom is impacted negatively. School leaders listen carefully to understand facts and perspectives presented by the teacher and parent involved. A school leader's role is to help both parties involved to come to a reasonable resolution together and not take sides. By helping parents and teachers resolve conflict respectfully, the interests of both parties are satisfied.

Recommended Guidelines and Protocol for Parents/Caregivers

- Request a conference as soon as an issue or difference of opinion arises.
- Speak to the teacher respectfully without anger or animosity.
- Enlist the assistance of the principal or an advocate if you are not comfortable meeting with the teacher alone.
- Make sure you understand your child's complaint or concern before approaching the teacher.
- Express yourself clearly and describe your position on the matter at hand.
- Refrain from sharing your issue or concern with your child/children and friends.

- Be open-minded and conduct yourself in a professional manner.
- Be able to communicate the rationale for your opinion or perspective on the issue.
- Provide relevant and specific examples that explain or describe your perspective, if needed.
- Remain calm and focused during the conference.
- Seek a resolution that is going to support your child/children.
- Be willing to agree to disagree.
- Avoid letting your personal feelings affect your relationship with the teacher and school.
- Keep the best interest of your child/children as the focus and outcome of your conference.
- Ask for clarifications, rationales, and explanations, if needed.
- Continue to communicate and support the teacher and school throughout the school year.
- Strive for a winning resolution for the situation.
- Address conflicts before they become crises and destroy relationships.
- Focus on collaboration, teamwork, and cooperation.
- Seek to understand and listen for a deeper understanding.

CHAPTER 5 SUMMARY

The items presented and briefly discussed in chapter 5 are areas/topics that often are points of confusion, frustration, or concern for parents in general. School administrators may have other topics or concerns that aren't present in this chapter. However, the areas that were presented have been the impetus for numerous conferences and disagreements between parents and teachers. Recommended guidelines and protocols provided give parents/caregivers specific steps and strategies to follow to make the transition easier and more understandable as they adapt/adjust to their school environment.

6

FOSTERING AND PROMOTING LIFE SKILLS FOR YOUTH SUCCESS

Many parents/caregivers are unaware of powerful life skills they have access to that help equip their children for life success. Parents/caregivers may be unaware of the fact that these powerful life skills, if fostered and developed from the time of birth, lay the foundation for future overall healthy living and wellness. All parents want their children to become successful and contributing members of society. The world today is ever-changing and growing rapidly. Youth need to be prepared and equipped with life skills to enable them to adapt, adjust, and modify or change direction as needed.

Exactly what are these life skills? How can they be fostered and developed at home? What must parents/caregivers do to ensure they provide the appropriate environment to nurture the life skills? Are there specific tips, guidelines, or techniques for these skills? Chapter 6 will present, discuss, and explore these selected life skills: self-confidence, self-esteem, resiliency, and perseverance. Parents/caregivers are given tips, suggestions, and guidelines to implement and lay the foundation to foster and develop the life skills that occur as children mature.

The importance and benefits of self-confidence, self-esteem, resiliency, and perseverance are shared. Also, since teachers are key players in the lives of youths, recommended classroom activities and tips are incorporated to increase teachers' awareness level and knowledge base about life skills for students. Chapter 6 is a roadmap and resource for parents as well as teachers and school administrators. Additionally, examples are included to illustrate several recommended tips and techniques for simple and easy implementation for parent/caregiver home use.

It is a well-known fact that parents are role models and living bill-boards for their children. Most parents are involved with their children's education and are comfortable helping with homework. Parents/caregivers who feel unequipped to assist with homework seek help from class-room teachers, tutors, older siblings, former educators, and online re-sources. Fostering and developing self-esteem, self-confidence, resilien-cy, and perseverance, however, is a different matter. Parents may not be aware and knowledgeable of the importance of life skills/traits for pro-ducing competent and emotionally healthy future citizens.

Youth learn, absorb, and glean information from their immediate envi-ronment and interactions with significant others in their lives as they grow and mature. The proverbial saying *Little pitchers have big ears* means be careful; children are listening. Not only are they listening, but they are watching too. Children acquire a wealth of learnings, experi-ences, and perceptions from their immediate environment prior to enter-ing school. For parents/caregivers to have a positive and meaningful im-pact, they need to begin laying the groundwork at birth. How can parents foster and develop life skills/traits at home? Why do life skills matter?

SELF-CONFIDENCE

Self-confidence is derived from a sense of competence. Children become self-confident when they have a positive and realistic perception of their abilities, capabilities, and accomplishments. Confidence is very important for youth's future happiness, health, and success in life. Confident chil-dren are better equipped to handle and deal with disappointments, chal-lenges, peer pressure, stress, responsibilities, and emotions (positive and negative). Where does a child's self-confidence and knowledge of his/her abilities come from? When does it begin? Who is key in starting the process of developing self-confidence in children?

Prior to the child enrolling in preschools, daycare centers, and schools, parents/caregivers are the most influential people in a child's life. What they say, do, or think affects their children's thinking and learning pro-cesses. Exposure to appropriate early learning experiences helps children acquire and develop a positive sense of confidence about their capabilities. During their early developmental stages and years, young children spend most of their time with parents and other significant adults. Fostering, promoting, and developing their children's self-confidence at home is not an intimidating and complicated task for parents.

Parents/caregivers can have fun and enjoy the process by implementing the following easy-to-do, researched-based, and effective strategies for building self-confidence.

1. *Ensure they know your love is unconditional.* Children draw a sense about themselves from how they are treated and viewed. They do not know they are cared for and loved until it is shown. The love that is shown by parents must be unconditional and sincere. Children need to know that they are still loved despite their mistakes and failures. Surrounding them with unconditional love helps them accept and realize they are worthy to be loved no matter what their capabilities are. Parents should avoid being overly critical, revengeful, unfair, or harsh when dealing with their children. Let children know you are a supporter and encourager who will remain with them for life.

2. *Practice positive self-talk with them.* Parents as well as children often find themselves engaged in negative self-talk such as *I can't do this, I am dumb, I have a hard time catching on.* They say negative things about themselves that are damaging, limiting, and hurtful. Sometimes we, as adults, pull ourselves down and weaken our self-confidence by making negative statements about our performance or actions. Remember, children do what they see and hear in the home. Parents/caregivers can model and encourage the practice of positive self-talk with positive affirmations.

   Following are recommended statements and affirmations parents/caregivers may use to replace the use of negative self-talk to build and strengthen self-confidence:

   - Mistakes help me learn and grow.
   - I haven't figured it out yet.
   - I am on the right track.
   - I can do hard things.
   - This might take time and effort.
   - I stick with things and don't give up easily.

- I strive for progress, not perfection.
- I go after my dreams.
- I cheer myself up when it gets hard.
- I am a problem solver.
- I try new things.
- I embrace new challenges.
- Learning is my superpower.
- I am brave enough to try.
- I get better at things when I practice.
- I grow my brains by learning hard things.
- I try different strategies.
- When I don't succeed right away, I try again.
- I ask for help when I need it.
- I learn from my mistakes.
- I focus on my own results and don't compare myself to others.
- I was born to learn.
- When I fail, I say I can't do it yet, and try again.
- I strive to do my best.
- I can learn anything.

3. *Address them by their name.* Simply calling a child by his/her name is a powerful way to show a child he/she is valued and important. In addition to calling children by their names, parents need to make friendly eye contact. Everyone likes to be called by their name and recognized as a person of value.

4. *Give them age-appropriate special tasks to do around the house.* Children feel like a valued member of a family when they are a contributing member of the household. Parents can assign children necessary age-appropriate chores to help them feel competent, responsible, and important. Being able to perform special assigned tasks gives children a sense of accomplishment and boosts their self-confidence.

5. *Join their play (and let them lead).* Spend time playing with your children. The mere fact that parents take time out of their busy day to play with their child/children sends a message of importance and worthiness. Letting them come up with an idea for a game and lead it gives them a sense of competence, well-being and confidence.

By accompanying and participating during children's play, parents are strengthening personal relationships with their children as well as increasing self-confidence.

6. *Focus on improving your own self*-confidence. Parents are walking billboards and role models for their children in the home. Take a quick assessment of your own level of self-confidence. If you find that your self-confidence needs repair, you may actively work on improving your own self-confidence by using positive self-talk and positive affirmations as a start. Refrain from using self-criticism in front of your children and model confidence instead.

7. *Ask them for their advice and opinion.* Asking your child/children for their help or advice on age-appropriate situations lets your child/children know you value their ideas and opinions. It also shows that even as an adult, you need help too. This demonstrates that adults do need help sometimes and it's fine to ask for help, if needed.

8. *Make special time together.* A key component of self-confidence and self-esteem is self-worth, which is demonstrated when parents spend quality and meaningful time with children. Setting aside time to do special projects, finding out their interests, sharing hobbies, having personalized conversations, and simply enjoying time together demonstrates their value and worthiness.

9. *Teach them how to set and reach goals.* Showing children how to set and achieve goals that are realistic is a great way for them to learn about their capabilities and build self-confidence. Under the guidance and direction of parents, children can select an age-appropriate goal to achieve and come up with a plan of action or steps to follow. Learning how to set goals not only gives youth a sense of independence, but it also gives them a strategy for keeping up with their accomplishments. As children achieve goals they have set for themselves, their sense of self-confidence and competence soars.

10. *Set aside time when you give them undivided attention.* Spending quality time with your child/children is needed to cultivate a sense of self-worth and value. To send quality time, parents need to set aside the time to spend with their child/children. This time needs to be free of interruptions and technology. Giving your full undivided attention during your time with your child/children is vital and necessary.

11. *Encourage them to try new things.* Children who are supported and encouraged to try new things often learn different things about themselves. Sometimes getting them to step out of their comfort zone will help them expand their abilities and skills. This new sense of confidence leads the way to extending their confidence and competence in other areas.

12. *Praise them the right way.* Don't praise children just for the sake of praising them. Telling them they're great and super when it's not true can give children a false sense of self-confidence and competence. If a child fails at something or shows little talent or skill, praise the effort, but don't be unrealistic about the result. Let children know it is okay not to be able to do everything perfectly. Some things improve over time with practice. Also, sometimes they should walk away and try or do something else after giving their best.

13. *Let them overhear you speaking positively about them to others.* Another quick and easy way to boost your child's/children's self-confidence is to let them overhear you *accidentally* talking about and sharing their accomplishments with others. Children are less likely to be skeptical about remarks they *overhear* than remarks you say directly.

14. *Resist comparing them to others.* Refrain from comparing your children to their siblings, friends, and others. Comparisons make children doubt their self-worth, value, and significance as a member of the family. They also doubt their abilities and feel they can't please parents or meet their expectations. These feelings erode their self-confidence, self-worth, and sense of competence.

15. *Cultivate their sense of belonging by hanging their portraits or artwork around the home.* Children gain a sense of belonging and self-worth when they see something that they had created or designed displayed in their home. The sense of love, belonging, and acceptance helps their self-confidence rise.

16. *Let them make age-appropriate choices.* Allow children to make choices and decisions such as what to wear, what to eat, where they want to go for an outing, what color to use, and so on. Children who make choices feel competent and powerful. Parents can also build choices in household chores and other special home-related tasks or activities.

17. *Help them discover their interests and passions.* Parents can assist children in discovering what they like or are passionate about through opportunities and experiences. By supporting the endeavors of their children, parents promote strengthening their skill or passion, which increases their self-confidence in themselves and the skill or activity.

18. *Help them overcome the fear of failure.* Fearing failure limits both children and adults. Parents who themselves are fearful of failure nurture and foster future adults who are fearful of failing. Because of the fear of failing, children are reluctant to take risks or venture out into new territory or ventures. This fear of failing eventually diminishes self-confidence and inhibits them from reaching their full potential. Parents can share their own struggles and others' failures in life and how persevering helped them overcome obstacles. Emphasis should focus on the fact that failing provides opportunities for growth.

19. *Encourage them to express their feelings.* Not acknowledging children's feelings and emotions may lead them to feel their feelings and emotions don't matter. To children, this means that they too don't matter. Encourage your children to express their feelings and emotions whether they are positive or negative. Assist your children in talking through their emotions and feelings in a healthy manner.

20. *Make sure they know you're not upset with who they are.* Children are children and will make the wrong choices from time to time. Remember they are still learning how to handle situations and may not solve problems appropriately. It is very important that children know that you still love them. Offer positive consequences and constructive feedback, not negative criticism or demeaning statements/remarks.

21. *Surround them with positive, confident people (including their friends).* If children are around positive, confident individuals, they have a better chance of becoming positive, self-confident individuals as adults. Parents need to be intentional in ensuring their children are surrounded by family and friends who will lift them up and not tear them down. This requires actively monitoring the friends and people allowed to be a part of their children's lives.

22. *Create a Wall of Fame to recognize their achievements.* Parents can demonstrate their pride and appreciation for their children's accomplishments by creating a wall or designating a spot to showcase work or successes. Children's efforts and determination can also be posted. Additionally, a Wall of Fame can serve as a reminder and confidence builder when children are experiencing struggles or obstacles with new endeavors or projects. Being able to view past achievements and accomplishments keeps their self-confidence intact and enables them to persevere despite obstacles.

23. *Shower them with hugs.* Communicate love, acceptance, and belonging to make your children feel happy and confident. Parents can give children high fives, pats on the back, hair tousles, back rubs, and loving squeezes that show they are care for and valued.

24. *Set rules and be consistent.* Children are more confident when they know who is in charge and what to expect. Even though your child or children may think you are strict, they will have confidence in what they can and can't do. The rules should be clear and consistently enforced. Also, the rules should reflect the beliefs, values, and principles of the parents' household.

25. *Coach relationship skills.* Being able to handle and deal with relationships impacts children's self-confidence. The first initial critical relationship they experience is a loving parent-child relationship. As children grow, the circle of relationships they experience expands outside the home. Parents will help their children see how their relationships affect others. It's their responsibility to help them maintain their inner self-confidence as their actions affect others. Parents must be mindful not to *fix* every situation. They need to teach children to handle the ups and downs of relationships with compassion.

Building Self-Confidence for Special Needs Children

Fostering and developing self-confidence as a life skill is important and critical for all children. It is important for parents/caregivers who may have children with learning disabilities to note that building self-confidence is paramount for special needs children. When they start attending school, they become very aware that maybe the way they learn is different and that it may require more time or repetitions for them to grasp a concept. Parents/caregivers help their child/children become more confident by recognizing and praising their efforts. Listed are additional specific tips recommended for parents of special needs children to build confidence:

1. Have open and honest dialogue with your child about his/her learning and thinking differences. Be a role model and willingly share some of your challenges. It's helpful for your child/children to hear how you value your own strengths and weaknesses.

2. For example, if you had difficulty remembering birthdays or items on a shopping list, share how you resolved the problem by saying, "I make a list before I shop" or "I write birthdays on my calendar to help me remember."

3. Give clear and constructive feedback. It is difficult for parents to be patient and not be critical when their child/children seem to be making little progress or when they have so far to go to improve. Parents must motivate them to continue trying and practicing without making them feel bad about themselves or their slow growth/progress.

4. Help foster a growth mindset. Train your child/children to reframe negative thoughts and statements about themselves. Encourage your child to develop a growth mindset believing in their ability to improve and learn over time and saying positive statements about themselves.

5. Teach your child/children that mistakes are learning experiences. Have them incorporate *next time* in their speech. For example, "I missed five of my words on the spelling test. Next time, I will practice and study my words longer, so I won't miss any spelling words."

6. Praise your child's/children's approach and effort, such as "I can learn" or "I will learn my multiplication facts in time." Children learn they are capable of meeting and overcoming obstacles if they are also praised for the self-initiated strategies and interventions.

7. Seek extracurricular activities that your child/children will enjoy and are good at. This helps them discover and appreciate their own strength and abilities.

8. Share and discuss the lives of successful role models who had learning disabilities and who may have experienced struggles in

school. Leaning about how others faced their challenges and prob-
lem-solved may inspire and motivate children to persevere.

Improving Self-Confidence in Classrooms

Teachers are seeing an increasing number of students in their classrooms
who lack or have low self-confidence. Many of these students who are
displaying this behavior are low achieving or students with learning exceptionalities. As a result of the challenges and struggles these students
encounter daily, they don't participate to hide their inadequacies from
classroom peers. Teachers or school administrators may see the behaviors
exhibited by these students as lack of motivation, laziness, uncoopera-
tiveness, or not working and trying hard enough. The truth is they are
trying but not achieving due to a learning disability.

Having low or no self-confidence is not an unusual occurrence for
children and youth with specific learning disabilities, motor skills, and
physical impairments. Also, special needs students along with lower-
achieving students may have difficulty expressing themselves when writing because of their limited vocabulary. Additionally, these students tend
to be disorganized, forget instructions, have difficulty following directions, and ask limited questions, if any, during class discussions/lectures.
They are labeled as troublemakers or nonconformist. Teachers, however,
can make a difference by building self-confidence in their classrooms.

Classroom teachers and school administrators can utilize simple tips
and recommended techniques that all students will benefit from regardless of their ability levels. These techniques and suggested tips require
hardly any preparation and materials. Boost self-confidence and your
classroom's/school's overall environment. They are designated below
with brief examples or explanations:

- Implement with integrity and fidelity all accommodations as specified in students' individualized education program (IEP).
- Encourage students to perform acts of kindness on a weekly basis.
- Praise all efforts and accomplishments made by students.
- Develop a communication system for students who are reluctant to
  raise their hand to ask for help. It can be as simple as a thumbs-up
  or placing a privately agreed-upon Post-it on their desk. *Note: This
  works well when signals are just between the teacher and student.*

- Listen objectively. Set aside a time when students may speak with you one-on-one about what is giving them difficulty.
- Plan service projects your students can do during or after school hours. For example, start a recycling club in your school, read to a kindergarten or first-grade class, and so forth.
- Establish and develop a classroom *Family* community. Encourage students to support each other. Promote a feeling of *we are in this together* among the students. Recognize birthdays and other special occasions in their lives.
- Develop a sincere and honest relationship with each student. Take time to visit their neighborhood (walk-throughs) to gain a better understanding of their home environments.
- Build trust and respect through your classroom rules and procedures.
- Set aside a check-in time in the morning for students to describe briefly how they feel.
- Offer choices and a variety of ways students can demonstrate their understanding of a concept/skill taught.
- Use the strengths of your students to tutor, mentor, or be a buddy for other students. Sharing a skill or an interest will help increase their self-confidence and perception of themselves.
- Emphasize the importance of continuing when some areas/topics may be a little difficult. Promote mistakes as opportunities to grow and learn.
- Start your mornings with positive affirmations or chants you or your students create to motivate and inspire everyone. Post positive and inspirational quotes around the classroom.
- Enlist the help of colleagues/students to serve as peer partners or mentors. Make sure the peer or mentor selected is respected and admired by the student they're working with.
- Expand your repertoire of techniques and strategies to engage students during classroom instruction.
- Celebrate successes and honor students for who they are.

School administrators have the ability and opportunity to help build the self-confidence of their entire student body including staff, faculty, parents, and community stakeholders. They are not only responsible for the total operation of the school, but they also set the overall climate and school environment. It is their leadership and expectations, values, and principles that set the stage for their school to be a nurturing and safe place for all constituents. They are entrusted with responsibility and tasked to employ staff who love, honor, and respect students and adults. They can utilize several tips recommended above to boost self-confidence schoolwide.

As an added feature for readers, I also included questions at the end of this section that may be used to generate open dialogue and reflective thinking about self-confidence. For self-confidence to be implemented and fostered with integrity, parents/caregivers and other significant adults need to work as a focused and intentional unit.

Questions to Think About (Self-Confidence)

1. What is my level of self-confidence? Do I need to improve?
2. Am I a positive model of self-confidence in my home for my child/ children?
3. Do I spend quality time with my child/children?
4. How do I encourage or support my child's/children's accomplishments?
5. Do I assign chores or special tasks based on the skills/interests of my child/children?
6. Do I make negative statements about myself or others in my household?
7. Have I encouraged or supported a passion or interest of my child/ children?
8. Have I used an idea or opinion of my child/children?
9. Are my rules consistent, age-appropriate, and fair?
10. What have I done to show my child he/she is valued and belongs?
11. How do I encourage my child/children to express feelings and emotions?
12. What positive affirmations do I want to use with my child/children?
13. Do I see failure as an opportunity to learn?
14. Which game(s) have I played with my child/children?
15. Do I spend one-on-one time with my children?
16. Do I use sarcasm to make a point?
17. Do I call my child/children names?

18. Do I intentional ridicule or embarrass my child/children?
19. Do I let my child/children know no one is perfect?
20. Do I expect/demand perfection?

SELF-ESTEEM

A positive self-esteem, like self-confidence, is vital for children to strive and survive as future adults in our challenging world. A healthy and positive sense of self is key to children's social, mental, behavioral, and emotional health. Like self-confidence, self-esteem is acquired and obtained from experiences, perceptions, sense of self, and feelings about our capabilities. Why is it important that youth feel *good* about themselves and *like* who they are? Also, why does it matter so much? What is the importance of self-esteem and how is it built?

Positive self-esteem indicates how individuals value themselves and how important they feel in their world. Parents/caregivers can start building strong and positive self-esteem at birth. The first step in fostering and nurturing self-esteem is creating an environment in which children feel safe and loved. The process begins when children are born and progresses over time. Loving care and attention parents/caregivers and other significant adults provide lay the foundation needed. Parents/caregivers have an ideal opportunity to lead their children on the way to academic success in school.

Self-esteem grows as children grow. Children feel better about themselves as they mature and can use their new skills. Parents promote their children's positive feelings about their capabilities by encouraging them to try things and learn skills such as holding a bottle, walking, playing peek-a-boo, riding a bike, talking, reading, and so on. Of course, the learning changes and increases as children grow and move through different intellectual, developmental, emotional, and physical stages. Parents showing children they're proud of their newly acquired skills strengthen children's self-love and worth.

Youth with positive self-esteems feel confident and capable. They are also proud of what they *can* do and always try to do their best. Youth who are confident about and like themselves for who they are develop a growth mindset. They accept frustrations and challenges confident they can succeed in the future. Children with positive self-esteem possess a *can-do attitude*. A growth mindset enables them to persevere despite obstacles and disappointments to achieve success.

Additionally, children/youth with positive self-esteem are more likely to speak up for themselves and request assistance or help if it's needed. Also, they motivate themselves to work hard toward meeting goals. By doing so, they continually increase their self-confidence and self-esteem as goals are reached and accomplishments increase. Accumulated successes help youth learn it's even okay to fail sometimes.

When youth have positive self-esteem, they:

- feel respected,
- are resilient and feel proud even when they make a mistake,
- have a sense of control over activities and events in their life,
- act independently,
- take responsibility for their actions,
- are comfortable and secure in forming relationships, and
- have the courage to make good decisions, even in the face of peer pressure.

Children who are not doing well in school and are not receiving positive feedback at home develop negative self-esteem and lack a growth mindset. They may not trust adults who have not been sincere and honest with feedback about their performance. In this instance, they mistrust the adults and their help. Lacking motivation to try things that are hard for them, children have a hard time handling or dealing with mistakes and failures. There is a belief that they may not be worthy of good treatment or success.

Youth with negative self-esteem may also:

- feel frustrated, angry, anxious, or sad;
- lose interest in learning;
- have a hard time making and keeping friends;
- be more likely to be teased or bulled;
- become withdrawn or give into peer pressure;
- develop self-defeating ways to deal with challenges, like quitting, avoidance, silliness, and denial; and
- have trouble developing strong self-advocacy skills.

Parents can help build and improve the self-esteem of their children at home by being supportive and encouraging. Down-to-earth parents with high and realistic expectations are needed instead of *overly protective* ones. Overly protective parents/caregivers limit their children's growth and development. Their well-meaning *interference* and *help* stifle creativity and block children's ability to learn how to problem solve and develop coping skills. Additionally, parents/caregivers should praise the efforts of their children but be careful not to lavishly praise *everything* they do.

For parents/caregivers of children with special needs, it is imperative that they focus on developing positive self-esteem. Children with learning and thinking difficulties are aware of the fact that many of their classmates are performing better without the difficulties they're experiencing. They work harder and sometimes longer to learn a skill or concept to progress and obtain success. Also, their learning exceptionalities may cause peers to avoid interacting with them due to their *inappropriate* behaviors. Other specific ways parents can help learning challenged children recognize, value, and use their strengths are:

1. *Open a dialogue and be a role model.* Talk to your children about what they think about how they learn and think. Share with them your own challenges and how you overcame them. Do not be afraid to discuss your strengths and weaknesses and how you value your abilities. For example, share your difficulty with remembering to purchase everything needed and how your problem-solving strategy of making a grocery list helped you.

2. *Provide clear but not critical feedback.* Addressing children sincerely and clearly about the challenges they face will motivate them to improve and not feel bad about themselves. Encourage them to work toward specific goals.

3. *Help foster a growth mindset.* Guide and assist children in reframing their negative thoughts and statements about themselves. Help them see how they can improve over time with appropriate practice. Champion their efforts.

4. *Teach that mistakes are learning experiences.* Assist your children in finding out what to do *the next time* to avoid making the same mistakes. Help them come up with a strategy or plan for trying another way to solve an issue or point out what they can do differently in the future.

5. *Encourage extracurricular interests or mentors.* Find extracurricular activities that your children enjoy without difficulty. Keep academic struggles in perspective. Increase their involvement and participation in activities that highlight their strengths. Or find individuals or stories about individuals who have had learning and thinking differences and were able to successfully use strengths/capabilities to overcome struggles.

6. *Point out successful role models with learning and thinking differences.* Knowing about other successful people such as athletes, actors, or celebrities and entrepreneurs with learning and thinking differences can be inspirational and motivating for children who are facing challenges. They will have the opportunity to learn how these individuals were able to accomplish different goals in their lives by not letting their differences limit them.

Improving Self-Esteem in Classrooms

Teachers have an integral role in in nurturing their students' sense of dignity and self-worth. Every student wants to do his/her best and be successful in the classroom. The reality of the situation is that not all students are successful or have pleasant experiences at school. Some of the factors are related to learning difficulties and low academic performance. Teachers and schools can help struggling students change their self-defeating mindsets and low self-esteem. To do so, a genuine desire to try to understand students' learning problems with positive interventions is needed.

Teachers and school administrators will need to recognize defeating behaviors students exhibit and refrain from administering punitive consequences instead of changing negative mindsets. Also, teachers need to recognize that behaviors such as acting like the class clown, quitting, saying they don't care, bullying, or not trying are ineffective coping strategies struggling students use. To help students improve their self-esteem, they must be taught in ways they learn best. Additionally, students need to be actively involved in their education. Appropriate interventions utilizing students' strengths increase self-esteem and self-value.

If teachers implement the key strategies below based on the specific students' needs, their students will develop a sense of ownership, control, and responsibility for their successes.

- *Demystify the problems.* The first step for teachers and school administrators is to appreciate the nature of the problems that students with low self-esteem and learning difficulties face. Help students discover and understand their strengths and weaknesses. Make instructional and program changes to accommodate their learning, learning styles, and social/emotional needs. Include parents, teachers, and all other stakeholders involved with the students daily. Include students and their self-evaluations/needs assessments as a part of the intervention process.

- *Utilize accommodations that maximize success.* Teachers that have students with IEPs should focus their instruction by incorporating the modifications and/or accommodations that increase their students' ability to learn concepts and skills presented. Create the opportunity for all students to thrive in the classroom. Spend time in the beginning of the school explaining all students have differences in learning. To meet those student differences, there will be different assignments, goals, and expectations for students based on individual learning needs.

- *Teach decision making and problem solving.* Teaching students decision making and problem solving are basic features of high self-esteem. Having the feeling of control over one's life improves students' ability to take ownership of where they are and what they do in life. Teachers can give students opportunities to make decisions and problem solve in classrooms. Allow them to make choices such as choosing a topic for a research project, deciding which assignment to work on from three to four choices, or telling a teacher what would help them learn a skill/concept better.

- *Utilize contributions of the students.* Students' self-esteem increases when they are aware of their contributions and do things for others and the world. Teachers and schools can plan avenues for sharing and caring for others in the classroom and school setting. Students can participate in drives to collect clothing and food for needy families, volunteer to help pick up trash on school grounds, run a school store, collect bottle caps, take care of plants in the building, and make cards for a local veterans chapter. Feelings of self-worth and value gained transfer over to academic skills.

- *Change mistakes mindset.* Teachers know that all students are concerned about making mistakes. Students with learning differences or low achievers are even more fearful of mistakes because of their difficulties. First, help by getting them to speak openly about their fear of failure before any mistakes are made. Involve students in an open discussion about what they, the class, and the teacher can do to minimize the fear of failing. Rules can be established about what to do or how to respond when they or a classmate doesn't know the answer. Open discussions lessen the fear of mistakes.

Questions to Think About (Self-Esteem)

1. Do I have a positive self-esteem?
2. Do I model a positive self-esteem in my home?
3. How do I encourage my child/children to love themselves?
4. Do I encourage independence?
5. Do I acknowledge and raise the efforts of my child/children?
6. Has my child exhibited admiration for his/her accomplishments?
7. Do my children set realistic and attainable goals?
8. Is my child able to stick with a task that may be difficult?
9. Can my child/children state their skills or capabilities?
10. Do my children welcome challenges?
11. Do my children request assistance or help readily?
12. How do my children handle mistakes or failures?
13. How do I help my children know their strengths and weaknesses?
14. What do I do to let my child know he/she is valued?
15. Do my children have a sense of self-worth?

RESILIENCE

How do youth overcome adverse childhood risk factors, such as poverty, divorce, physical and sexual abuse, and other situations, and still manage to become productive contributing citizens? Also, despite struggles and setbacks, they reach long-term goals and bounce back from disappointments. Researchers believe that some children have higher levels of resilience that account for their success with life. Resilience is the ability to bounce back from everyday life challenges. Resilient children are described as having determination, toughness, optimism, faith, and hope.

Children who are resilient face and handle the uncertainties of childhood with determination. The good news is that parents can have an active role helping children develop resiliency. There is no way to protect youths from experiencing some of the adverse encounters such as substance abuse, physical and emotional neglect, divorce, mental illness, incarceration, homelessness, and death that may enter their world. Being resilient does not exclude children from experiencing stress, frustration, hopelessness, or sadness over a loss and change in their family dynamics. Resilient youths work through obstacles. Resilient youths survive.

Resiliency is not a skill that children either have or don't have. It's a coping skill that children develop as they grow. Children who are resilient are more likely to take risks without the fear of falling short of expectations. They are curious and brave and trust their own instincts and abilities. Knowing their limits and capabilities, resilient youths are willing to step outside their comfort zone. Parents, on the other hand, have the tendency to protect their children from neighborhood bullies, disappointments, and other stresses they may face. Overprotective parents limit children from developing resiliency and coping skills/strategies.

Chatterjee (2019) is concerned about the rise in young people's mental health problems. Pressures range from school stress and bullying to worries about jobs and housing prospects. She states that the brain responds to information around us, which enables resiliency to be taught through modeling and nurturing at any age. According to Chatterjee, parents do not need to overhaul parenting styles to foster resiliency. A little tweaking of what they do currently will help children thrive. Resiliency comes from relationships children have with the significant individuals in their lives. Parents/caregivers should incorporate and implement the following tips to nurture and raise resilient children:

1. *Have one-on-one time with each child.* Quality is better than quantity. Parents don't need to carve additional time out of their busy day or hectic schedule. Make use of everyday times such as bath time, mealtime, grocery shopping, homework time, and so on. During these activities, listen, talk, ask questions, share your feelings, and encourage them to express their feelings. Once the one-to-one times become regular, children will know they a safe space to freely communicate.

2. *Give sleep a chance.* Many children are struggling to sleep and waking tired with dark circles under their eyes. A lack of good quality sleep is a huge case of stress. Monitor time viewing devices and enforce specific bedtimes. Viewing screens before bed keeps us emotionally wired and stimulated.

3. *Get out and exercise.* Regular exercise is important for everyone. Children need even more exercise. Try to have bursts of exercise throughout the day. Exercise not only keeps children, as well as adults, physically fit but also increases resilience by strengthening the brain. Regular physical exercise teaches our stress response system to recover more efficiently.

4. *Teach delayed gratification.* Learning and understanding that you can't have everything you want is resilience too. It's an important concept to pass onto children. People who can accept delayed gratification lead healthier and happier lives. Without this ability, children are missing a key component for their well-being. Parents can use board games that require impulse control, turn taking, and mental flexibility. It is also a good way for parents to model resilience by being a good loser.

5. *Good nutrition impacts mental health.* Good-quality food helps send calm signals to the brain. A diverse diet, rich in fiber, leads to greater variety of the gut bugs in the stomach, which makes us more resilient and anxiety and depression less likely. The entire family can play the game Eat the Alphabet and cross off the letters in thirty days by eating twenty-six plant foods: A for asparagus, B for banana, C for chickpeas, and so on.

6. *Model gratitude.* Teach children to reframe their day without pestering them with questions. Instead, children can be encouraged to find and look for positives during the day.

Questions to Think About (Resilience)

1. Have I modeled resilience for my child/children and family?
2. What experiences can I share that demonstrate ways I've been resilient?
3. What strategies do I currently use to help recover from disappoints or setbacks?
4. Does it take me a long time to bounce back from failure?

5. How do I conduct myself when things don't happen as I expect?
6. What is or has been my biggest failure?
7. How did I feel and cope with that failure?
8. Did I change as a person as a result of the failure or disappointment? If so, how?
9. What will I do differently the next time I face failure or disappointment?
10. How do I avoid making drama out of crises?

PERSEVERANCE

Teaching children to persevere is not an easy task for parents. Perseverance, however, can be taught. It is a skill or trait that allows someone to continue trying even if the struggle is long term. Being able to push through difficulties and see things to the end is even a difficult task for adults. How can parents/caregivers teach children about the benefit of not giving up and hanging in there no matter the effort or cost? Children, as well as adults, encounter day-to-day struggles of persevering through hard work. There are goals in life that take years to come to fruition. Parents may see raising children or completing high school as events requiring perseverance.

When youth are challenged, overwhelmed, and frustrated, they have the tendency to shut down, experience high levels of anxiety/stress, or give up. Parents/caregivers can foster the development of perseverance by being a model for children. Children learn from their environment and the significant adults in their lives. Parents can lead by example, demonstrating and sharing how they persevered and tackled challenges in their lives or on their jobs. Children as well as adults benefit from the ability to put forth the necessary effort needed to accomplish a goal or task despite obstacles, unexpected changes, and disappointments.

Parents/caregivers should have frequent discussions with their children about the importance of persevering when a task is difficult or a new learning. Teaching them to respond positively to a change or setback will guide them in responding and designing alternate plans. Lessons about the importance of persevering can be taught at home, school, or elsewhere in the community. Children can begin the process young and will become stronger and more adept as they learn ways to pick themselves up after falling. Being able to persevere is more important than possessing a high IQ. Children and adults need more than academics.

Parents/caregivers may incorporate and include the recommended tips below with their parenting practices to foster perseverance at home.

- *Encourage children to make try new things regularly.* Parents may want to try new things with their child/children. No one is perfect when they start something new. This new activity can be turned into a family affair such as skiing or skating. Let them see that not winning or falling is not the end of the world.
- *Make connections.* Teach children/youth how to make friends, including the skill of empathy, feeling the pain of others. Encourage children to be a friend to make friends. Being able to connect with others provides social support and strengthens perseverance and resiliency.
- *Adjust the degree of perseverance needed.* If children need a small challenge, present an activity they already know or have abilities in. If a larger challenge is needed, have them participate in an activity that is out of their comfort zone. Be sure the activity is age and developmentally appropriate.
- *Be overt and tell them they are going to work on some perseverance skills.* Let them know that they may struggle and could possibly fail. Knowing a task or activity is hard ahead of time makes it easier to deal with the difficulty.
- *Be there for them if they do struggle or fail.* Provide support and help them to evaluate to determine why things were not successful. Were there any additional supports needed? Guide them in determining how to plan and try again.
- *Recognize effort and don't reward/celebrate their achievements only.*
- *Help children find their passion.* Parents often decide what their children's interest will be. Allowing them to pursue their own interest/passion will motivate them to practice. They'll be engaged and work hard to do what's needed to persevere for success.

Improving Perseverance in Classrooms

Educators realize that students need more than academic content to live successful lives. Schools are focusing on equipping students with social and emotional skills to face the challenges of life in the twenty-first century. Teachers and school personnel can better prepare students for the future by providing them with learning experiences and class/school activities that will promote perseverance and other related coping skills such as grit and resiliency. The greatest gift teachers and parents can give is a *growth* mindset. Teachers can help children learn that their talents and abilities can be developed through effort and persistence—perseverance.

Like resilience, teachers can encourage students to not give up but continue to strive to move forward. Students that believe they can't learn/improve or have control over their learning or action have a *fixed* mindset. To promote and encourage growth mindset development in classrooms, teachers should:

- Be mindful of the messages they send to their students thorough their words and actions.
- Provide activities that require them using perseverance to complete.
- Have discussions with students about what they do to keep themselves motivated to accomplish long-range goals.
- Brainstorm as a class ways or strategies to keep them from giving up.
- Help them to understand that learning isn't easy all the time.
- Instruct students on how to set realistic, attainable goals.
- Design problem-solving activities for them to resolve as a whole class or small group.
- Discuss and share appropriate ways to handle frustrations, disappointments, and failures.

Questions to Think About (Perseverance)

1. What has been the biggest obstacle I've had to overcome in my life or career?
2. What steps did I take when faced with the obstacle?
3. What steps or plan did I put in place to overcome the obstacle?

4. How did I motivate myself to not give up and continue?
5. Did I ask for advice, seek resources, or request assistance to work through the task?
6. Did I design a plan of action? If so, was it successful and why?
7. Did I learn any lessons that I can apply to other areas of my life?
8. Did I acquire any new skills, knowledge, or insights about myself while going through the struggle?
9. How do I maintain optimism during difficult tasks and times?
10. Am I open to trying new experiences that are difficult or take a long time to complete?

CHAPTER 6 SUMMARY

Self-confidence, self-esteem, resilience, and perseverance are four powerful tools that youth as well as adults need to help them live productive and successful lives. In this chapter, I briefly described each skill/trait and their benefits. Parents/caregivers are given tips and recommendations to encourage them to foster and nurture the development of these powerful tools from birth through adulthood. Each of the skills can be taught and learned with proper guidance, experiences, and intentionality. Parents/caregivers play a key role in establishing and equipping children with skills/traits that will extend through adulthood.

Teachers, next to parents, are also very influential in the lives of youth. Suggestions, tips, and recommended strategies are provided for each of the four coping skills presented in chapter 6. Teachers can nurture and reinforce the skills in classrooms. The tips and strategies shared require little or no preparation for teachers to implement effectively. Also, several examples are included that specifically illustrate what teachers can use to meet the needs of students that have learning differences or are low achievers. Teachers are encouraged to use students' strengths to plan and design appropriate interventions based on how students learn.

Following each coping skill/trait shared, questions for readers to think about and generate discussions are included. The purpose of the questions is for parents/caregivers, teachers, and school leaders to evaluate/assess where they are in the process of fostering and promoting these skills in the home and educational setting. By being supportive, focused, and intentional, parents/caregivers, teachers, and school leaders work together as partners collaboratively preparing and equipping youth with tools to help ensure life success.

Chapter 7 serves as a resource listing of specific games and instructional activities for parents/caregivers and teachers to use in homes and classrooms. Readers will be able to select a game or activity for each coping skill presented in chapter 6: self-confidence, self-esteem, resilience, and perseverance. Families may use the games and activities to grow and develop as a family unit. Also, many of the games and activities listed are appropriate for teachers to implement in classrooms.

7

GAMES AND INSTRUCTIONAL ACTIVITIES TO BOOST LIFE SKILLS FOR YOUTH SUCCESS

This chapter consists of a listing of games, instructional activities, and brief ideas for parents/caregivers to use at home to help encourage, foster, and promote the development of self-confidence, self-esteem, resilience, and perseverance. These games and activities may also be used by teachers, childcare centers, daycares, preschools, community organizations, and churches. Instructions are provided and materials are listed, if needed. My main purpose for this chapter is to provide hands-on activities for easy use. All children need to develop these coping life skills to reach their full potential and have successful lives.

THAT'S WHAT I LIKE ABOUT YOU: SELF-CONFIDENCE AND SELF-ESTEEM

This activity may be conducted during a casual meal or family gathering. Take turns going around the table saying one nice thing about each other.

A PICTURE SPEAKS ABOUT ME: SELF-CONFIDENCE AND SELF-ESTEEM

Material(s) Needed: Old magazines or pictures downloaded from the Internet and printed.

Instructions: Cut out a variety of pictures displaying actions (skiing, swimming, running, sewing, painting, baking, reading, etc.). Display the pictures on a table. Each person selects a picture (one or two) that shows an interest or something he/she is passionate about. Individuals take turns sharing (talking about) their interest. *Note: Pictures for this activity may be downloaded from the Internet. This is an excellent activity for teachers to use to get students to introduce themselves.*

WHO AM I?: SELF-CONFIDENCE AND SELF-ESTEEM

Using a small brown paper bag, family members cut out four pictures or place objects that represent them in the bag. Family members must guess who the person is and tell why the picture or object represents the individual. Or individuals may suggest additional pictures or objects that represent the person and tell why they chose that object or picture.

WE ARE FAMILY: SELF-ESTEEM, SELF-CONFIDENCE, AND PERSEVERANCE

Material(s) Needed: Chart or poster paper, pencils/pens, and tablet (optional).

Instructions: Brainstorm a list of volunteer activities or projects the family can do together for the neighborhood and/or community. Assign family members different responsibilities for the activity or project. Together the family develops a plan and timeline for the tasks needed to complete the activity or project. A chart may be created to show the family's progress.

FIVE THINGS I LIKE ABOUT MYSELF: SELF-ESTEEM AND SELF-CONFIDENCE

Material(s) Needed: A plain sheet of lined or unlined paper; a pen/pencil, crayons, or markers.

Instructions: Using a sheet of plain paper, ask your child/children to write or draw five things they like about themselves. Children do this activity without suggestions from adults or friends. When they complete the activity, direct them to tell you why they chose the qualities or pictures. If your child/children have difficulty naming or saying what they like about themselves, spend time helping them increase their self-esteem. You may also reread/review chapter 6 or seek additional resources. *Note: This a variation of the Mirror Mirror activity.*

MIRROR MIRROR (AGES 4–10): SELF-ESTEEM AND SELF-CONFIDENCE

Material(s) Needed: Hand mirror, plain paper, assorted crayons/magic markers, and pen/pencil.

Instructions: Using a small hand mirror, direct your child to look at him-/herself for a few seconds (15–20). Ask*: What do you see?* (Accept all responses.) *Name four or five things you like in the mirror. Draw a picture of or write down what you like about yourself on a plain sheet of paper. Note: Young children who are unable to write may tell you what they like about themselves.* Refrain from telling your children what to say or write about themselves. The activity can be extended for older children by asking them to share *why* they like what is listed. If your child/children have difficulty thinking of what they like about themselves, tell them what *you admire/like* about them (personality, character traits, skills, etc.).

COMPLIMENT CIRCLE: SELF-ESTEEM AND SELF-CONFIDENCE

This game provides practice for giving compliments to family members and friends. A minimum of six children need to participate.

Figure 7.1.   Example of a hand mirror.

Material(s) Needed: A clear area in or outside.

Instructions: The children sit in a circle on the ground or floor facing each other with their legs stretched out in front of them. Select someone to begin the game by giving someone a compliment. The person that received the compliment folds their legs crisscross and chooses someone to compliment.

INVENT A RECIPE: SELF-CONFIDENCE, SELF-ESTEEM, AND PERSEVERANCE

Help your child/children see mistakes as opportunities for learning, not failures. Try this activity and provide a gentle situation for making a mistake.

Material(s) Needed: Determined by the recipe the child *invents*.

Instructions: Ask your child/children to invent their own recipe for pancakes. Have them write down an ingredient list and the quantities of each item. *Note: Young children may dictate their recipe to a parent/ caregiver or an older sibling.* Supervise the process so nothing dangerous is ingested, but do not interfere with the recipe. If your child adds something unusual to the recipe (like goat cheese or garbanzo beans!), let them experiment. After cooking a test batch of pancakes, ask if there is anything they would do differently. Allow your child/children to modify the recipe and try again.

I AM ACTIVITY: SELF-CONFIDENCE AND SELF-ESTEEM

Is your child proud of his/her achievements or accomplishments? Does he/she like him-/herself? Find out by playing this game.

Material(s) Needed: Drawing or poster paper; cutouts of adjectives (words) from magazines; glue; sheets of plain writing paper; photo of your child; colored pencils, crayons, or markers.

Instructions:

1. Ask your child to list words on a sheet of paper that describe him/ her. The words can be negative or positive.
2. Next, ask him/her to focus on the good things people have said and list them.
3. Paste the photo in the center of the drawing paper or poster paper.
4. Ask your child to fill the area around his/her photo with positive words and adjectives that describe him/her.
5. Place the completed chart in his/her room to reinforce positive beliefs about themselves. *Note: Words may be added as positive beliefs continue to grow.*

6. Lead your child to turn the negative statements into positive ones. The statements should be clear and specific to the talents and abilities of the child. *Note: Start the activity by giving an example of a negative statement you made about yourself and turn it into a positive statement. Share how the positive statement helped you.*

LISTING WINS IN LIFE: SELF-ESTEEM AND SELF-CONFIDENCE

Material(s) Needed: A sheet of plain paper or small notebook and a pencil or pen.
Instructions:

1. Give your child the sheet of paper or notebook.
2. Have your child write down their successes for that day. Leave enough space to write down additional successes as the day progresses.
3. Have your child review their list at the end of each day. Daily listings of successes remind children that they can do something and be successful.

VISUALIZATION: SELF-ESTEEM, SELF-CONFIDENCE, AND RESILIENCE

Material(s) Needed: A quiet and calm area or place to relax.
Instructions:

1. Find out why your child thinks he/she is not good or what he/she is afraid of doing.
2. Focus on whatever they are afraid of or fear. For example, if he/she is worried about a performance in a sport, focus on that.
3. Ask your child to imagine and write down what the ideal scenario would be.
4. Next, ask your child to close his/her eyes and imagine the ideal scenario and how he/she would feel if it was real.

5. Ask him/her to write down how he/she felt when the ideal situation was visualized. *Note: Encourage and train children to visualize themselves succeeding and thinking positive about themselves.*

CHANGING SELF-TALK: SELF-ESTEEM, SELF-CONFIDENCE, AND RESILIENCE

Material(s) Needed: A sheet of a paper and a pen or pencil.
Instructions:

1. Make two columns on a sheet of paper. On one side, write *Bad or Negative Self-Talk* and on the other side write *Good or Positive Self-Talk.*
2. Ask your child to write down all the negative statements he or she makes under the *Bad Self-Talk Column.*
3. Next, ask your child to turn the negative statements into positive ones. The statements should be clear and specific to the talents and abilities of the child. *Note: Start the activity by giving an example of a negative statement you made about yourself. Change it into a positive statement. Share how the positive statement helped you.*

I AM AFRAID, BUT ... : SELF-CONFIDENCE, SELF-ESTEEM, RESILIENCE, AND PERSEVERANCE

Material(s) Needed: A sheet of paper and pen or pencil.
Instructions:

1. Ask your child to list the things he/she is afraid to do; for example, fearful of talking in front of his/her classmates, going to swimming class, trying out for the cheerleading, or asking someone out on a date. The sentences should begin something like this: "I am afraid to speak in front of my class because . . ." "I am afraid to go to swimming class because . . ."
2. Next, tell your child to imaging doing the very thing they fear.
3. Try to develop a *so what* mentality. For every fear written, they write what some possible outcomes could be if they tried what is

feared. Next to any negative outcome written, they write, "Even if I get rejected, so what!"

CATCH THE COMPLIMENT: SELF-ESTEEM AND SELF-CONFIDENCE

Material(s) Needed: An indoor or outdoor play space large enough to accommodate the players (make sure no breakables are nearby). Soft, lightweight balls (various sizes: e.g., beach balls, foam balls, playground balls).
Instructions:

1. Gather the players in a circle.
2. Players take turns tossing one ball to someone different in the circle. As each toss is made, the player tossing the ball gives the receiver a compliment.
3. The receiving player then tosses the ball to someone else, again giving a compliment as the ball is released.
4. If desired, gradually add more balls as play continues. This will increase the pace and the level of challenge to the players as they think of compliments to give.
5. At the end of the game, take the time to ask players what the hardest, easiest, and funniest aspects of the game were for them. Ask them to explain what they had to do to be successful.

MAKE SLIME: SELF-CONFIDENCE AND SELF-ESTEEM

Material(s) Needed: See recipe for Slime.
Instructions: Assist your child/children with the recipe for slime (listed below). After the slime is made, ask them to explain the process to you. Invite their friends or family members over! Your child becomes a presenter and demonstrates the slime-making activity to others. *Note: Other simple recipes or craft projects may be used.*
Easy Slime Recipe

- Mix 1/4 cup water with 1/4 cup of glue (Elmer's or other name brands).
- Add a few drops of food coloring (their choice) and 1/4 cup of liquid starch.
- Knead the slime until it is pliable.

FEELINGS JOURNAL: RESILIENCE, SELF-ESTEEM, AND PERSEVERANCE

Material(s) Needed: A small tablet or notebook.

Instructions: Children record their feelings daily. They evaluate their day and jot down, for example, what happened that made them feel happy, sad, nervous, and so on. At the end of the day, they review their feelings and come up with strategies to help them block negative feelings and increase *good* feelings.

PROUD OF ME: SELF-ESTEEM AND SELF-CONFIDENCE

Materials Needed: None.

Instructions: Gather students in a large or small group. Students stand up, face the group, and state a reason why they are proud of themselves. This activity can be done while students are sitting at their desks or table. It's also an excellent introduction activity for starting a new grade or being in a new place. By everyone participating (including the teacher or adults), everyone begins to see the value of others. This activity can be adapted for use with elementary, middle, and high school students.

BRAINSTORMING: RESILIENCE

Material(s) Needed: None.

Instructions: Encourage your child/children to bounce back and problem solve when unexpected things happen. Use everyday situations that occur. For example, "I wanted to wear my favorite shirt to the party. It's dirty!" Say, "What can you do?" Let them come up with alternatives.

I CAN AND I AM CUP GOAL SETTING: SELF-ESTEEM, SELF-CONFIDENCE, AND PERSEVERANCE

Material(s) Needed: Three 5-inch plastic or Styrofoam cups, craft popsicle sticks, a black marker or pen, index cards (plain or lined), glue or scotch tape, and three 2x4-inch plain mailing labels.

Instructions:

1. Write on the mailing labels *I Am*, *I Can*, and *My Goals* and place the labels on the cups.
2. Cut index cards into strips wide enough to write on with a marker or pen.
3. Tell your child to write brief sentences that describe or tell something about them and tape or glue them onto a craft popsicle stick. Place them in the *I Am* cup.

Figure 7.2.   Example of needed materials.

4. Next, tell your child to write what their skills, talents, and traits are. *Note: Refrain from telling your child what to write.* Place them in the *I Can* cup.

5. After the sentence strips are completed, briefly discuss what they wrote. Ask if there is anything they want to learn or improve. Their responses become goals. Extend their thinking and goal setting with the sample questions below (optional).

Possible Questions to Guide an Action Plan

- What can you do to improve your spelling grade?
- When is your next test? How many days do you have to study?
- How long do you want to study?
- Is there anything you need do differently to improve? If so, what?
- Do I need to help you study? If so, how?
- What do you think may help you learn how to spell your words?
- Which words do you already know how to spell? *Note: Author designed.*

TRUST WALK/OBSTACLE COURSE: RESILIENCE AND PERSEVERANCE

Material(s) Needed: Outside area safe area. *Note: Any number of children can play.*

Instructions: Children are partnered. One person in the team is blindfolded. The other partner guides his/her partner through a self-made obstacle course by giving them directions, support, and advice. Children rely on what their partner tells them to get through the obstacle course. They also learn how to trust each other.

CALMING STRATEGIES: RESILIENCE

Material(s): None

Instructions: Teach your children strategies to calm themselves when they become angry or upset such as taking deep breaths, counting to ten, listening to soothing music, or muscle relaxation.

SOMETHING ABOUT ME: SELF-ESTEEM AND SELF-CONFIDENCE

Material(s) Needed: A sheet of paper and a pencil or pen.
Instructions: Write the prompts below on the paper. Tell your child/ children to complete the sentence prompts below.

- My friends think I am awesome because . . .
- My classmates say I am great at . . .
- I feel very happy when I . . .
- Something that I am really proud of is . . .
- I make my family happy when I . . .
- One unique thing about me is . . .

HULA-HOOP CHALLENGE: RESILIENCE, PERSEVERANCE, AND PROBLEM SOLVING

Material(s) Needed: A Hula-hoop.
Instructions: Children form a circle holding hands. Before the last pair connect, place a Hula-hoop over one arm. Without letting go of each other's hands, they should move the Hula-hoop around the circle. Children will have work together to move the hoop and support each other so they don't fall. When the game is over, talk about what made the game difficult and the ideas they came up with to solve problems.

PERSONAL RESILIENCY JOURNAL: SELF-CONFIDENCE AND SELF-ESTEEM

Material(s) Needed: A tablet or notebook.
Instructions: Children keep a record of how they handled a situation that was challenging for them. They briefly note what they did to handle the situation and how they felt. This also will serve as a reminder that they can work through situations and will maintain their self-confidence and self-esteem.

MUSICAL CHAIRS: RESILIENCY AND PERSEVERANCE

Material(s) Needed: Chairs and music.
Instructions:

1. Walk around the circle of chairs when the music starts.
2. Find a chair to sit in when the music stops.
3. Leave the game if you're left without a chair.
4. Remove a chair and play again.
5. Continue playing rounds until there is one person left (winner).
6. Children share their emotions at the end of the game.

PICTURE PUZZLES: RESILIENCE, PERSEVERANCE, AND PROBLEM SOLVING

Material(s) Needed: A picture puzzle and small envelopes.

Instructions: Put one or two pieces of a puzzle in an envelope. Make sure you have enough puzzle pieces to distribute among the participants. Have children open their envelopes one at a time and place their puzzle piece(s) on the table. The object of the game is to put the puzzle together as a team. After the puzzle is completed, the children share any difficulties experienced.

STORYTELLING: RESILIENCE AND PERSEVERANCE

Material(s) Needed: None.

Instructions: Parents/caregivers share their childhood experiences. Talk about your struggles and how you overcame them. Include times you weren't resilient. They learn from your experiences too. It is good to share that you have struggles too. Use the questions below to help guide your story/sharing (optional).

- What happened?
- Why did you do what you did?
- When and why did you give up?
- Is there anything you regret doing?

- Did you learn anything new about yourself?
- When was the turning point for you?
- What strategies did you use to handle the situation?

CHORES WITH A PURPOSE: SELF-CONFIDENCE, SELF-ESTEEM, AND PERSEVERANCE

Material(s) Needed: A sheet of poster paper, pen or pencil.

Instructions: Make a list of meaningful age-appropriate chores your child/children can do around the house. Compliment your child/children every time a chore is completed successfully.

VISION/DREAM BOARDS: RESILIENCE AND PERSEVERANCE

Material(s) Needed: Old magazines, crayons, poster board or poster paper.

Instructions: Children visualize where or what they want to be in the future. They cut out or draw pictures that represent their future. Encourage them to set goals. Then talk about what they need to do to make their dream/future a reality.

RESILIENCE INTERVIEWS: RESILIENCE AND PERSEVERANCE

Material(s) Needed:

Instructions: Encourage child to interview grandparents, neighbors, or other acquaintances who have worked hard to reach a long-term goal. Make sure the individuals interviewed share their struggles and what they did to reach their goal(s).

MOTHER AND DAUGHTER ACTIVITY: SELF-ESTEEM

Material(s) Needed: Poster or chart paper (4), crayons, or assorted markers.

Instructions: On one set of posters, write *Me* and *My Mom.* On the other set of posters, write *Me* and *My Girl.* The daughter writes positive things on the *Me* and *My Mom* posters. The mother writes positive things on the *Me* and *My Girl* posters. *Note: This same activity can be used by sons and both parents.*

FAMOUS PEOPLE STUDY: RESILIENCE AND PERSEVERANCE

Material(s) Needed: Books about famous people who have triumphed over obstacles.

Instructions: Encourage children to study and discuss how famous people overcame failure and didn't give up; for example, Michael Jordan, Jim Carrey, and J. K. Rowling. These examples will show children that resilience and perseverance through failure can lead to success.

LITERATURE STUDY: PERSEVERANCE AND RESILIENCE

Material(s) Needed: Classic stories from literature such as *The Little Engine That Could* to help children make connections to their own life.

Instructions: Read and discuss the story with your child/children.

I AM GRATEFUL NOTEBOOK: SELF-CONFIDENCE, RESILIENCE, AND PERSEVERANCE

Material(s) Needed: Notebook or small tablet and pen or pencil.

Instructions: Children begin or end their day by writing down what they are grateful for. This activity will help them focus on or think about the good/positive things happening in their lives.

THINGS I CAN'T DO YET: SELF-ESTEEM, SELF-CONFIDENCE, RESILIENCE, AND PERSEVERANCE

Material(s) Needed: A sheet of paper or poster, pen or pencil.

Instructions: Draw or fold the paper to make three vertical columns. Write in the first column *Things I Can't Do Yet*; in the second column, *Steps Needed to Learn*; and in the third column, *Date Goal Accomplished*. Children develop a plan to monitor their own growth and add new goals. They take ownership of their learning and connect their efforts with goal completion.

RANDOM ACTS OF KINDNESS: SELF-ESTEEM AND SELF-CONFIDENCE

Material(s) Needed: Drawing paper, crayons, assorted colored pencils or markers, and pen or ink.

Instructions: Children make cards and write kind messages inside the cards to give to siblings, family members, neighbors, or classmates. They may also make cards for a senior citizen facility in their community.

WALL OF FAME: SELF-CONFIDENCE AND SELF-ESTEEM

Material(s) Needed: Poster paper, pen or pencil, crayons or assorted colored markers.

Instructions: Children make a list of their accomplishments or things they are proud of. They may also draw pictures representing how they feel about their successes. Hang or post the paper where it will be a daily reminder and motivator.

LET'S SNAP IT!: RESILIENCE, PERSEVERANCE, AND PROBLEM SOLVING

Material(s) Needed: A sheet of paper, pen or pencil.

Instructions: Respond (in writing) to the statements below. This activity allows for family collaboration on issues or challenges that may occur.

Statements:

- *S*ay the problem (write a brief description).
- *N*ote the outcome desired.
- *A*cquire possible solutions.
- *P*inpoint top one and do it.

GOOD-BYE TO WORRY: RESILIENCE, PERSEVERANCE, SELF-ESTEEM, AND SELF-CONFIDENCE

Material(s) Needed: Jar or small cardboard box (shoebox), several 3x5-inch plain or lined index cards, and a pen or pencil.

Instructions: Children write what they are worried or anxious about and three things they can say to themselves to let go of the worry or anxiety. After placing the card in the jar/box, they repeat at least one of the statements written throughout the day. Once the worry/anxiety is lessened, the card is thrown away.

WHAT I CAN DO TO NOT FEEL UPSET: RESILIENCE AND PERSEVERANCE

Material(s) Needed: A tablet or notebook, pen or pencil.

Instructions: Children keep a log of things they can think about or do to keep from getting upset. They may also note which of the logged ideas or things work the best for them.

WHAT IS THE HARD PART?: RESILIENCE AND PERSEVERANCE

Material(s) Needed: None.

Instructions: When child/children want to give up because something is *hard*, ask, "What's the hard part?" Discuss and identify the challenge and ask what he/she can do to fix or overcome the hard part. Refrain from giving your child/children the answer and guide their thinking.

THE GRIT PIE ACTIVITY: PERSEVERANCE

Material(s) Needed: Paper plate, pen or marker. Recommended for older children/students.

Instructions: Draw lines and divide the paper plate into six slices. Each child writes a difficulty/problem they are having in each slice. Lead the child to discuss the obstacle and decide the problem is temporary or permanent. The three steps for this activity are:

1. Identify the problem (the pie).
2. Slice the pie. Each slice is a different cause to the problem.
3. Categorize the problem. *Note: Problems categorized as temporary are within his/her control.*

MY POSITIVE THOUGHTS AND WHAT I CAN DO TOMORROW: SELF-ESTEEM, SELF-CONFIDENCE, RESILIENCE, AND PERSEVERANCE

Material(s) Needed: Notebook or small tablet, pen or pencil.

Instructions: On a sheet of paper, children write the positive thoughts that they had that day.

On the bottom of the same page, they write one to three plans for the next day. They check off daily the plans they completed for the next day.

READING BOOKS: SELF-CONFIDENCE, SELF-ESTEEM, RESILIENCE, AND PERSEVERANCE

Material Needed(s): Age-appropriate related books about self-confidence, self-esteem, resiliency, and perseverance. Visit your local library and request assistance.

Instructions: Read the stories and guide discussions with questions.

BOUNCE BACK AT SCHOOL: RESILIENCE, PERSEVERANCE, SELF-CONFIDENCE, AND SELF-ESTEEM

Material(s) Needed: None. *Note: This activity is excellent for teachers to use in classrooms.*

Instructions: During a math lesson, if the majority of the students get a problem wrong, divide them into small groups to find the correct answer to the problem together. Select students to share how they corrected their mistakes. Students learn that others make mistakes too.

CHAPTER 7 SUMMARY

These selected games and instructional activities were provided to give parents/caregivers and teachers a repertoire of coping skills activities to use at their convenience. Many of the activities included address one or more of the coping skills presented in chapter 6. It is hoped that parents/caregivers will be encouraged and motivated to extend the list by adding additional activities. This resource is not all inclusive, but there are enough games and activities shared to have an impact on children, families, and classrooms if they are utilized with intentionality and consistency.

CONCLUSION

Writing this resource handbook has been a labor of love and commitment. With more than forty years of experiences as an administrator in an elementary school, I saw many changes and trends come and go. One thing that has not changed is the importance of and key role parents play in laying the foundation for their child's/children's learning. There are many factors and variables that impact children's lives. As educators and school leaders, we must continue to reach out to parents/caregivers and other stakeholders to enlist their help and expertise to enable all children to reach their full potential.

This resource handbook was written to encourage and empower parents/caregivers and community stakeholders to collaborate, engage, and partner with their schools. Together we are stronger and can achieve more. We all have a stake in equipping youth with the tools needed to enable them to live healthy, productive, and successful lives.

BIBLIOGRAPHY

Adams, Caralee. "What the Research Says about the Best Way to Engage Parents." Hechinger Report, February, 2020. https://hechingerreport.org/what-the-research-says-about-the-best-way to-engage-parents/.

Anderson, Carly. "10 Questions Every Parent Should Ask at an IEP Meeting." The Mighty, September 2016. https://themighty.com/2016/09/questions-every-parent-should-ask-at-an-iep-meeting/.

Ayyoub, Laureen. "National Teacher of the Year Shares 6 Tips to Help Parents Empower Their Child in the Classroom." *Good Morning America*, September 2019. https://www.goodmorningamerica.com/family/story/national-teacher-year-shares-tips-parents-empower-child-55013356.

Bernhardt, Victoria. "No Schools Left Behind." *Educational Leadership* 60, no. 5 (2003): 26–30. www.ascd.org/educational-leadership-/feb03/vol60/05/No-Schools-Left-Behind.aspx.

Brown, Patricia Clark. "Involving Parents in the Education of Their Children." KidSource, Inc., August 2019. http://www.kidsource.com/involving-parents-education-their-children.

Calderon, Valerie L., and Jefferey Jones. "Superintendents Say Engagement, Hope Best Measures of Success." Gallup, September 2018. https://www.gallup.com/education/243224/superintendents-say-engagement-hope-best-measures-success.aspx.

Chatterjee, Rangan. "Six Ways to Raise a Resilient Child." *The Guardian*, January 2019. https://www.theguardian.com/lifeandstyle/2019/jan/05/six-ways-to-raise-a-resilient-child/.

Clavel, Teru. *World Class: One Mother's Journey Around the Globe in Search of the Best Education for Her Children*. New York: Simon & Schuster, 2019.

Cullins, Ashley. "9 Activities to Build Grit and Resilience in Children." *Big Life Journal*, January 2020. https://www.whitbyschool.org/passionforlearning/6-self-esteem-activities-to-help-your-child-develop-confidence.

———. "25 Things You Can Do Right Now to Build a Child's Confidence." *Big Life Journal*, September 2017. https://biglifejournal.com/blogs/blog/child-confidence.

Education World. "Activities to Promote Parent Involvement." Education World, May 2017. https://www.educationworld.com/a_curr/curr200.shtml.

Fitzpatrick, Jean Grasso. *Once Upon a Family: Read Aloud Stories and Activities That Nurture Healthy Kids*. New York: Penguin Inc., 1998.

Fries, Daniel. "12 Simple Activities You Can Do to Start Building Self Esteem Today." Psych Central, October 2018. https://psychcentral.com/lib/12-simple-activities-you-can-do-to-start-building-self-esteem-today/.

Fuller, Cheri. "Helping Your Child Succeed in Public School." Illinois Tyndale House Publishers, 1999.

Goldberg, Sally. *Make Your Own Preschool Games: A Personalized Play and Learn Program.* Cambridge, MA: Perseus Publishing, 2002.

Gongala, Sagari. "8 Simple Activities to Build Self-Esteem in Children." Mom Junction, July 2019. https://www.momjunction.com/articles/increase-self-esteem-in-your-child_00357511/.

Hernandez-Sanabria. "Engaging Families in Early Childhood Education." RTI Network, 2017. www.rtinetwork.org/essential/family/engagingfamilies.

Hiatt-Michael, Diane. "Parent Involvement in American Public Schools: A Historical Perspective 1641–2000." *School Community Journal* 4, no. 2 (Fall/Winter 1994).

Keith, Kimberly L. "How Parents Can Become More Involved in Schools." Verywell Family, July 2019. https://www.verywellfamily.com/parent-involvement-in-schools-619348.

Kelly, Melissa. "Parent Role in Education Is Critical for Academic Success." ThoughtCo., February 2019. https://www.thoughtco.com/parent-role-in-education-7902.

Kirkwood, Donna. "Understanding the Power of Parent Involvement." NAEYC, April 2014. https://www.naeyc.org/resources/blog/understanding-power-parent-involvement.

Logsdon, Ann. "A Game to Boost Your Child's Self-Esteem." Verywell Family, July 12, 2019. https://www.verywellfamily.com/develop-self-esteem-with-interactive-games-2162838

Lyness, D'Arcy. "Your Child's Self-Esteem." KidsHealth, July 2019. https://kidshealth.org/en/parents/self-esteem.html.

Maroney, Diane. "7 Tips to Teach Kids/Students to be Resilient." The Imagine Project, March 2019. https://theimagineproject.org/teaching-kids-students-to-be-resilient/.

Mead, Sarah. "6 Self Esteem Activities to Help Your Children Develop Confidence." Whitby School, December 2019. https://www.whitbyschool.org/passionforlearning/6-self-esteem-activities-to-help-your-child-develop-confidence.

Meador, Derrick. "Why Principals Must Relationships with Parents." ThoughtCo., December 2016. https://www.thoughtco.com/why-principals-must-build-relationships-with-parents-395617.

Medhus, Elisa. *Raising Children Who Think for Themselves.* New York: Fine Communications, 2001.

Morin, Amanda. *The Everything Parent's Guide to Special Education.* New York: Adams Media, 2014.

———. "7 Ways to Help Your Child Develop Positive Self-Esteem." Understood, December 2019. https://www.understood.org/en/friends-feelings/empowering-your-child/self-esteem/7-ways-to-boost-your-childs-self-esteem.

Moss, Wendy, L. "Helping Your Child Learn to Bounce Back." Magination Press Family, August 2015. https://www.maginationpressfamily.org/stress-anxiety-in-kids/helping-child-learn-bounce-back/.

Reinke, D. Dana. "What Do Parents Do When You Don't Like Your Child's Teacher." Today's Parent, October 2016. https://www.todaysparent.com/kids/what-to-do-when-you-dont-like-your-childs-teacher/.

Shultz, Jerome. "I Am What I Choose to Become." *Attitude Magazine,* September 2019. https://www.additudemag.com/teaching-resilience-to-adhd-children/.

Sledge, Bria. "Empowering Children Is the Way to Go." Very Important Parent, April 2017. http://www.bevip.org/uncategorized/empowering-children-is-the-to-go/.

Uddin, Lilufa. "Family Ties: How to Get Parents Involved in Children's Learning." *The Guardian,* February 24, 2017. https://www.theguardian.com/teacher-network/2017/feb/24/parents-involved-school-teaching.

Waterford UPSTART. "How Parent Involvement Leads to Student Success." Waterford, November 2018. https://www.waterford.org/education/how-parent-involvment-leads-to-student-success/.

Wood, Lacy, and Emily Bauman. "How Family, School, and Community Engagement Can Improve Student Achievement and Influence School Reform: Literature Review." Nellie Me Education Foundation, February 2017. Nmefoundation.org.

ABOUT THE AUTHOR

Sheila E. Sapp has devoted forty-four years to education, learning, children, and families. She has served as a classroom teacher, assistant principal, curriculum director, and principal during her career as an educator. Sheila recently retired from the Camden County Schools System as principal of Crooked River Elementary School, located in St. Marys, Georgia. Her school was recognized as a 2002 School of Excellence and a Title I Rewards School for High Academic Achievement for five consecutive years (2012–2016). Dr. Sapp is the former cofounder of Sapp and Bruce Educational Consulting, LLC. She currently has her own consulting business, Sheila E. Cares Educational Consulting and Services, LLC.

Dr. Sapp is a graduate of the University of Georgia with an education doctorate degree in supervision and curriculum. She holds a master's in reading education (K–12) from Glassboro State College (now Rowan University) in Glassboro, New Jersey, and an education specialist degree in administration from Georgia Southern University. She has authored three books, *The Learning House, Best Practices for New School Administrators*, and *Staying the Course: A Guide for Best Practices New Administrators*. Additionally, Sapp has conducted workshops for teachers and parents on conferencing and motivating students. Dr. Sapp copresented at the National Youth At-Risk Conference, March 10, 2020, in Savannah, Georgia. She resides in Woodbine, Georgia, with her husband, Everette.